Rediscovering the
A Holy Grail

The elusive Holy Grail—was it the Kiddush Cup with which Jesus celebrated the Last Supper, or only a figure of speech for a long-sought spiritual objective? *Evoking the Primal Goddess* proposes that it is neither, and it provides evidence that may very well put an end to speculation on its mystical nature.

The Holy Grail as a topic of discussion will be familiar to almost every student of the Western esoteric tradition, yet no one *until now* has ever dared to suggest what it was as an objective. William Gray explains exactly what the Christian Holy Grail was, why it was of such importance to medieval Christians, and why it is still so vitally important to all who inhabit the Earth today.

In the old days we would have said that no male God concept would possibly be complete without its specific Goddess, nor a Goddess concept adequate without its correct counterpart. Gray shows that the search for the Grail is really the search for a matriarchal principle of Deity. By matching all our Deity concepts in ourselves, we can create the ideal Mystical Marriage, which is the ultimate aim of all esoterically minded students.

How can we as individuals find a personal, meaningful, *living* feminine aspect of Deity? In *Evoking the Primal Goddess*, Gray provides us with fascinating and simple techniques, rituals, and prayers that will help men and women alike to evoke a personal image of the Mother Ideal, as well as *invoke* her so that we can join the two polarities into a spiritual concept of practical power.

About the Author

William G. Gray was born in Harrow, Middlesex, United Kingdom. His mother was an astrologer and psychic consultant. He comes from a long line of churchmen, with his heritage extending back to Archbishop Walter de Gray of York, one of the founders of its famous Minster.

He received much of his early training in the Western Inner Tradition from an associate of Papus. This individual was a Qabalistic Rosicrucian, and Gray believes that his writings were profoundly influenced by this person's teachings. Gray is the author of many highly acclaimed books, including *Ladder of Lights, The Inner Temple,* and *Between Good and Evil.*

To Write to the Author

We cannot guarantee that every letter written to the author can be answered, but all will be forwarded. Both the author and the publisher appreciate hearing from readers, learning of your enjoyment and benefit from this book. Llewellyn also publishes a bimonthly news magazine with news and reviews of practical esoteric studies and articles helpful to the student, and some readers' questions and comments to the author may be answered through this magazine's columns if permission to do so is included in the original letter. The author sometimes participates in seminars and workshops, and dates and places are announced in *The Llewellyn New Times.* To write to the author, or to ask a question, write to:

William G. Gray
c/o THE LLEWELLYN NEW TIMES
P.O. Box 64383-271, St. Paul, MN 55164-0383, U.S.A.

Please enclose a self-addressed, stamped envelope for reply, or $1.00 to cover costs.

LLEWELLYN'S NEW WORLD MAGIC SERIES

The European re-discovery of the "New World" was much more than a geographic confirmation of the "Lands to the West."

For the members of various esoteric groups, America was to be the "New Atlantis," a utopia free of ignorance, superstition, fear and prejudice—incarnating a Great Plan for the spiritual evolution of this planet. Central to the political foundations of this *New Order for the Ages* is the intellectual freedom to pursue knowledge and wisdom unrestrained by the dictates of Church and State, and to publish and speak openly that all the people may grow in wisdom and attainment.

At the very core of this vision is the recognition that each person is responsible for his or her own destiny, and to freely pursue this "Happiness" requires that one throw off domination by "personal devils" of psychic nature, just as the American Colonies rebelled against the despotism of the British King.

We must be free of that which hinders our Vision and obstructs the flowering of the Life Force. For each of us that which obstructs is our *inner* personal Evil, and it is the Great Work of the magician to accept responsibility for that Evil and to transmute its powers into personal Good. Therein lies the secret of spiritual growth.

And with personal transformation comes our enhanced Vision and Power to work with magical responsibility in the outer world and to transmute those Evils resultant from human ignorance and fear, superstition and prejudice. We move forward as we perceive such Evils as originating from within ourselves and as we challenge them in their true nature.

We live in perilous times, but a "New Age" is at hand as the techniques of personal magic are used by more and more people to accept responsibility for Evil, and to redeem it for the Good— for individual growth and success, and for the Good of the planetary life within which we have our being.

New World Magic is visionary, recognizing the role of the individual practitioner in the world in which we live, and accepting the promise of a "New Order for the Ages." It is magic that is psychologically sound and spiritually committed. It is magic that builds upon older traditions in the knowledge that within them are our roots, and it is magic that looks to new understanding to ever expand the potential into which we grow.

New World Magic is for all who want to make a *New World*!

Other Books by William G. Gray

Between Good and Evil
Temple Magic
The Ladder of Lights
Magical Ritual Methods
Inner Traditions of Magic
Seasonal Occult Rituals
The Tree of Evil
The Rollright Ritual
An Outlook on Our Inner Western Way
A Self Made by Magic
The Talking Tree
Western Inner Workings
The Sangreal Sacrament
Concepts of Qabalah
Sangreal Ceremonies and Rituals

Forthcoming

Sangreal Tarot (tentative)
By Standing Stone & Elder Tree
Attainment Through Magic

Llewellyn's New World Magic Series

Evoking the Primal Goddess

Discovery of the Eternal Feminine Within

William G. Gray

1989
Llewellyn Publications, Inc.
St. Paul, Minnesota, 55164

International Standard Book Number: 0-87542-271-3

First Edition, 1989
First Printing, 1989

Cover Art: N. Taylor Blanchard

Produced by Llewellyn Publications
Typography and Art property of Chester-Kent, Inc.

Published by
LLEWELLYN PUBLICATIONS
A Division of Chester-Kent, Inc.
P.O. Box 64383
St. Paul, MN 55164-0383, U.S.A.

Printed in the United States of America

To my wife Roberta (Bobbie)
This book is dedicated in loving gratitude.

Table of Contents

Introduction

To all of you:

There is a very old legend that says swans sing before they die, which means that before we quit this world we should leave something pleasant behind for people to remember us by. Well, here is my swan song, which amounts to the music of my whole life compressed into a few bars.

It took me this entire incarnation to learn what you can read in perhaps less than a day, although it will take you a lot longer than that to make anything of it. Most of my time was spent learning my lessons the hard and bitter way, so remember that when you read this. I suppose the real question is, Do I think these were worth learning, and would I gladly go through it all over again? Yes I do, and maybe not so gladly, but I'll still have to come back and pick up all the points I've missed during this lifetime. I only hope I can find as understanding a mother in my next incarnation as I had in this one (God rest her soul). One of my great regrets is that she never lived to read anything I ever wrote, even if much of it would have meant little to her as subject matter, though I'm sure she would have liked this one. She cared about whatever I did because I was part of her and we both belonged to the same esoteric tradition, which she served in one way and I in another.

As they say, a person can have only one mother. It is a unique relationship in this life, although a very long time ago most of us believed that we all came from the same Great Spiritual Mother, whom we knew by endless different names depending upon which language we spoke, and even today we call this our mother tongue. It is good to think that a growing awareness of our common Mother is coming back to us in these times. Children fight amongst themselves, as every mother knows, and we silly humans have had our squabbles and surely ought to be old enough by now to behave like grownup human beings. After all, we are one family of brothers and sisters whatever we may think of each other as individuals, and at the moment we've only one world to share between us, so why not do that sensibly? We may be on the verge of exporting ourselves elsewhere to continue the Sangreal story, but we might as well leave here in peace while there is still a little prosperity left.

Anyway, here is my finding of our Great Mother, and I hope with all my heart it might help at least some of you to gain an improved awareness of Her. Now all I've got left to say is farewell, and may my love and blessings be with you. I won't say goodbye, because I've always felt it sounded too final, and I know we'll meet up again somewhere and somehow. May we all find our greatest happiness together where everything began: in our beloved Bloodbeing's most wonderful womb.

—Wm. G. Gray (Bill)
A.E. 1988

Chapter One

Our Feminine Fundamental

A recently known but inadequately publicized fact is that all human beings are fundamentally feminine. At an early stage of our fetal development, every one of us is a female. One hormone alone makes males different: testosterone. This converts what would have been a clitoris into a penis, and in consequence the embryo becomes a male human creature. Conversely it is another hormone, estrogen, which converts the otherwise infertile female into an egg producer. Were it not for this fact of basic biology, we would have the same kind of society as our ants and bees, one in which the bulk of beings would be nonfertile females caring for the eggs produced by a single Queen-Human, the eggs having been fertilized by the relatively few males reserved for this task alone. These "flock females" would also be responsible for the culture and behavior of our species in general.

So the old story of Eve being cloned from Adam should really be reversed. Our order of precedence ought to begin with Eve, from whose womb we are supposed to have sprung. Esoteric legend says that so far as sexed cellular life is concerned, this began in the ocean, our oldest Mother, and those cells that floated nearest the surface and were mainly influenced by the Sun's rays became males, while those that lived on lower levels but were still subject to the pull of the Moon stayed female. That certainly aligns with our instincts, which subsequently led us to develop the Solar and Lunar cults of our Deity ideologies, all the patriarchal and matriarchal cults resulting therefrom, and the combinations and transcendencies arising from the union of both.

What we can gather from our past prehistory tells us that at first human society in general was mainly matriarchal. It was the women who bore the children, cared for them, clothed and instructed them, and were responsible for the amenities of home life and the associations of humans as a family or tribe of people. Women were the herb and plant gatherers, the weavers, the collectors, and probably the earliest agriculturists, since they tended to locate their homesteads around the plants they cared for. It is more than likely that women originated the first human ideas of Deity or of any supernatural states of existence apart from our normal conditions of living. As humans, females have a natural tendency to internalize, whereas males will externalize. This could be because the female organs of generation are internal, while the male ones project externally. Therefore any ideas of Deity that came to female human minds in primitive times would have taken some "Goddess-shape" in the simplest kind of Bringer-forth-of-Life concept.

Men, the externalizers, were projective in nature and confrontative in character. Being herd creatures, they fought for what they wanted, whether this happened to be females, food, or territorial rights. Seeing that each of them had grown from the union of a single sperm, which had survived amongst millions of others in the race for a solitary egg, they carried on the same aggressiveness throughout their active lives as adult humans. They were the hunters and explorers, searching for new territory to occupy or females to fertilize. If they ever formed any ideas of Deity, it would be in their own image, magnified to the extent of their ambitions; or ideologically, a God with the power to push himself into people and persuade them to accept whatever he offered. In other words, one who functioned as a sort of superphallus in a superior way. It is interesting to reflect that the ancient Hebrews considered themselves female in relation to their Deity, and they consequently called it to mind in masculine guise.

The upshot of all this was that as the human race evolved and bred into distinct genetic variations, so did each variety formulate and define their own specific types of ideology and thinking processes until these became genetically imprinted into their offspring. In the end, ideas by themselves survived much longer than those people who had formulated or first thought of them, because they were virtually written into the cells from which we were built up in our mother's wombs. Considering what can be electronically etched into a silicon microchip in our times, it should surprise no one to presume what might be possible with living cells that have been part of previous people or their conscious culture. Every single molecule or atom that once formed part of our human life-chain has an infinitesimal impression of its past experiences indelibly attached to it, and ultimately after extensive reuse it becomes a factor of increasing importance in our evolutionary progression. Even the waste matter we excrete from our bodies becomes valuable fertilizer, which is then taken up by the vegetable kingdom and so promotes our living in one way or another. Nothing in life-energy is ever lost, but only altered and reapplied elsewhere. To die in one form is to be reborn in another.

Whatever happens on physical levels of life has its equivalent on spiritual ones also. In fact, many mystics believe that the reverse is the true order, and that inner spiritual experiences precede or foreshadow their material counterparts. It is certain that we cannot physically act without thinking about it first, even if this thought takes only a split-second or is an almost automatic procedure. If we can extend that principle for mere moments, we can extend it indefinitely, and can thus consider a situation that has taken a thousand and more years to think out or appreciate. That is the way our God concepts arose. They were born from many millennia of thinking and feeling—first the female Mother-God, and then with the spiritual equivalent of testosterone, the male Father-God.

At that stage we would not have realized that our God-beings were magnifications of ourselves and our natural propensities to a degree considered Divine. In fact, this is beyond the comprehension of many contemporary mortals. Put as simply as possible, if every human female who had ever lived were combined together to make up one single Woman, there would be our ideal Goddess, and in the case of males, there would be our ideal God. Combine the best of the two together correctly, and that would present an idealized Individual. Project the thinking further until the eventual end of our evolution, and we would come to the goal of our Godhood, which is the perfection of Power as PERFECT PEACE PROFOUND. A blending of both our male and female polarities into a single spiritual Individuality of infinite intelligence and endless energy, or in other words, the sort of God we would not only want to worship, but better still, want to *become*.

Our concepts of Deity evolved from an inherited or genetic instinctual belief that some greater power than any possessed by individual humans was influencing the course of our collective lives from some unknown state of existence, and connecting with ours by equally unknown means. At first we recognized this mysterious Energy as a maternal influence, and later as a paternal Being. We formalized our relationship with whatever this power might be with religious ritualism and pious practices, subsequently extending our connection to philosophical, moral, and ethical areas of awareness. Efforts were made by pantheists, who mixed male and female God concepts with specific approaches to either, and by deists, who saw their versions of supreme Beings as pure power and above sex altogether. There were also the nonreligious, who saw no need for beliefs in any kind of entity, yet agreed it would be best for humans to live by common codes of conduct in reasonable accord with one another. Up till our present period there does not seem to have been sufficient agreement amongst the humans of our world to prevent all possibilities of conflict and the consequent destruction of civilized conditions upon our Earth.

A great proportion of the blame for such a situation could rest with those who have allowed our world to become a male-dominated society guided by masculinized Gods that originate from controlling angles of consciousness and cover the widest areas of human awareness. Although the feminine factor has by no means been absent from our superior spheres of influence, it has scarcely exercised enough effort to equal that of its masculine counterpart. In theological terms, our Gods have proved stronger than our Goddesses so far as pure Power is concerned. The results of this in terms of warfare, brutality, violence, and human horrors of all kinds have been too obvious and memorable to avoid notice. Be it particularly noted that in recent history such shocking events have been chiefly amongst the male-dominated regions of this world, where the official religions are mainly Christian or Muslim, both deriving from the Hebraic concept of a predominantly masculine God.

From a purely spiritual and remote viewpoint this kind of domination could be interpreted as a type of rape, or forced intercourse, between unwilling Goddesses and Gods who were seeking no more than their immediate sexual satisfaction regardless of results. The principle is beautifully mythologized by the story of Athena and Vulcan, when the latter attempted to rape her. He failed to make complete penetration and discharged his seed outside her womb, which the Goddess then wiped off with wool and flung to Earth, where it produced nothing but monsters. One of these was Erichthonius, reputed to have serpents' tails instead of legs, and who was credited with inventing the war chariot drawn by horses. The horse, it may be remembered, was produced by Poseidon as his contribution to humanity during his famous contest with Athena for dominion of Attica. Athena produced the olive tree, and hers was judged by the Gods to be the best article because it would result in peaceful and profitable trading, whereas the horse would bring only warfare and bloodshed.

While Athena (whose name means The Deathless One) was recognized as the Goddess of warfare, this was taken to mean solely in the case of unavoidable warfare, in which all efforts at negotiations or compromise had failed. She was also assumed to have equal power with her father, Zeus, from whose head she was born fully grown and armed. In her we have a Goddess concept of equal efficacy to that of maximum masculinity, and a spiritual supporter of peace, intelligence, culture, and everything that makes life worth living. A special point to note, however, is that she was never portrayed as any kind of a Mother figure, or as being in any way superior to man (although his complete equal in every possible sense). As a nonreproductive female, she would represent the ideal denizen of an insect-style community centered around a solitary mother-parent whose endless eggs would be fertilized by a minority of males maintained for that function alone. That would sound suspiciously like a dream-world concept of our modern militant feminists, except that our biological factors would scarcely permit such a thing at present.

Human history and destiny, however, are determined by our Deity concepts, whatever they happen to be. Our Gods may not necessarily be our personifications of powers or natural energies at all. They might equally well be our ideas of whatever we believe to be of primal importance in our lives. With most mortals this means themselves surrounded by a supportive circle of enhancing adjuncts such as friends, money, social importance, sexual interests, and similar mundane concerns. The literal meaning of "God" is "whatever is worshipped," while "worship" is derived from the old term "worth-ship," or one's true evaluation of anything. In other words, whatever we value most highly or account most precious to ourselves. So, strictly speaking, the term "divine worship" means showing what we consider our ideas of Deity to be really worth. It is surely significant that in many of our churches or places of worship, the central focal item is a large collection plate for the offering of money, which is the real object of worship in these temples of mammon, the money-God of every era.

If the average human believes in a God of any sort, it is usually considered as a Giver, a supreme source from whence may be obtained whatever may be demanded; or an extension of parent-providers magnified into metaphysical spheres of importance. First the Mother concept, from whom comes life, sustenance, shelter, comfort, and care, then the Father concept offering experience, training, excitement, stimulus, and wherewithal. We sometimes refer to our God concept as Providence, meaning a great universal Provider wherefrom we may gain the guerdons we would have from It during our lives on this planet. In short, a "gimme" God. To that extent our Deity concepts have scarcely advanced at all beyond those of our earlier epochs, and many might be forgiven for supposing they have regressed very considerably indeed.

At some very primitive period of our past it could have been that our remotest male ancestors did not consciously associate the sex act with childbirth nine months later. Earlier Australian aboriginals are known to believe that they "caught" babies from natural phenomena, such as bushes or strangely shaped stones encountered during their walkabouts, while sex practices were no more than pleasant physical experiences indulged in at intervals during moments of mutual desire. The chances are that males were only seasonally fertile in remote prehistoric times, and this coupled with a low vitamin intake made male impregnation an occasional rather than a regular result of sexual intercourse. This would naturally be noticed first by the females, who noted the cessation of their Lunar blood flow during prebirth periods, and so the conscious connection was made between blood and birth. They might not know which of the males was responsible, and so the natural assumption would be made that it was all of them who had intercourse prior to the cessation of blood flow. It is probably for this reason that earlier civilizations took their lines of descent from their mothers rather than from presumptive fathers. Jews keep up that tradition to this very day.

With the development of tribalism and the formation of families, males began to rule their societies by force of strength rather than by subtle persuasion. That was essentially a feminine faculty, which women soon learned how to use so as to circumvent or alter the rule of men should that become insupportable, and so the females played their part in the subsequent structure of human society. However much men may have resented this, they had to accept a proportion of Goddess deities among their spiritual superiors. For that matter, they were quite willing to respect, revere, and especially fear their shamanesses, who showed evidence of abnormal intelligence when they prophesied deaths or placed curses on men whom they quietly poisoned afterwards. Some of their sayings might even have been genuine psychic promptings from inner areas of a common subconsciousness, which were then presumed to be the Gods themselves in person. All such contributions either assisted or retarded our rates of progress along their average lines.

Whether this fact seems acceptable or not, it is our Deity concepts that determine our ultimate destiny as a species, both from an individual and a collective standpoint. They form the directive force in our lives—the "Divinity which shapes our ends, rough hew them how we will." They are our long-term concepts, which being genetic and consequently inheritable, outlast any single human life and affect the whole course of our history indefinitely. As we ideate our Deities, so will they determine the sort of beings we shall become, and what we are really looking at through our beliefs in Deity is ourselves as we truly want to become in our furthest future. It is interesting to note the scriptural words attributed to Satan in Genesis when he spoke to Adam and Eve concerning the results of eating the forbidden fruit from the Tree of Knowledge. "Ye shall be as Gods, knowing good and evil." That is literally true. We shall become as the Gods we believe in, both good and evil, because those are the control concepts that direct our eventual becoming.

When humanity realized that it had opposing propensities in itself—some of which could be classed as good, to be fostered and encouraged, while the contrary ones were to be discouraged or abrogated as evil or undesirable—we did what was then the sensible course of action: set up Gods to cover both contingencies. So a good God was conceived at one end of the scale, and an evil One was permitted its place at the opposite position. They were really diametrically opposing polarities of the same Power, inseparable by sheer necessity as the positive and negative polarities of our Lifeforce. From thenceforward we would have our Deity-Devil concept to work with, both drives serving the same cosmic circuit. Its good end being what we should evolve *towards*, while the evil end was what we should evolve *away from*. At least that gave us a sense of direction as existing entities (or it should have done). Unluckily, there would always be a proportion of humanity that developed an alternative sense of balance and so took a turn towards the evil end of the Lifelevel. The great majority of humankind, however, have swung between the two extremities for many millennia, and so we are brought to our present point of so-called civilization, where we now hang on our most modern mark.

Naturally, the clearer, more decisive and definite we can make our God concepts, and the greater confidence we can place in them, the more effective and influential they will become. To what extent modern people believe in their Deities is extremely questionable. There is a sarcastic story told of a boatload of illegal immigrants bound for Britain that was suddenly caught by the most terrible storm in which all seemed doomed to perish. They were urged to pray for assistance from the most powerful British God they could think of, and in less than seconds they were all prostrate repeating: "O Great National Assistance save us! O Great National Assistance save us!" A similar tale is told of a Scot in a parallel position. When others were calling on every God they could think of for help, he remarked casually, "Well if I've got to do something religious, I'll just take up the collection." Mammon, or *maymoun*, from whose name our word "money" is derived, remains one of humankind's oldest and most popular Gods. In fact it is puzzling why in America, where a new religion is being invented almost every day, there has not yet appeared a Church of the Almighty Dollar, wherein the object of worship would be an enormous representation of a bank note. It would at least have the virtue of honesty, since humankind might as well acknowledge what it worships most, and mammon certainly comes first for a great many people.

The fact is that we have let our God concepts deteriorate to a point where they have become so diversified and uncertain as to be almost useless in formulating our Lifefaith. Every so often we have been accepting an Avatar as a guide to our next collection of religious or ethical beliefs—such as Zoroaster, Buddha, Confucious, Moses, Jesus, or Mohammed (all of whom advocated much the same principles under different formularies)—and have altered our outlooks accordingly. It is almost as though each one of those humans reached and realized a completely different condition of consciousness than that available to the ordinary mortal, and managed to convey enough of it back to our ordinary levels whereon it acted as an inspiration to keep us occupied for several centuries. The question is whether it can survive as a spiritual stimulus much longer, or to what extent we need a new impetus that will successfully carry us past this dawn of our Nuclear Age.

In our times we have not as yet encountered an Avatar capable of convincing our consciousness as to the validity and practical application of acceptable God concepts, or else we have met far too many of them to cope with comfortably. Could this be because the majority of our previous faith-foci have been male, and that we are instinctively awaiting a female Figure who will gratify our genetic demands for Deity? Or is it because the Christ concept is appearing in so many messiahs at once that we cannot tell which if any should be preferred over the others? Alternately, are we still awaiting some Supersoul capable of synthesizing our present plethora of spiritual speculations into a single convocation of consciousness that we cannot fail to recognize as authentic evidence of our Godhood?

Perhaps all these postulations are true and definitely necessary to the present conscious condition of most people living on this planet. Maybe our greatest need is for the actual presence among us of a Deity concept that not only guides our living but is fully capable of caring for our souls beyond any boundaries that death may limit our individual cell-lives with. We need as a common commodity the sort of faith that Carl Jung was expressing during his last interview before a camera. He was asked whether he believed in the immortality of the human soul and its survival past death. With a very strange sort of smile, he replied quite slowly and very deliberately, "I do not have to believe, I *know*." Such was the strength of his certainty.

As an internationally recognized medical specialist in his own field, Jung dared not allow his private convictions to become public knowledge for fear of being discredited by the authoritarians of his day. Science at that time had to deny the least suspicion of spirituality or the slightest possibility of Deity, except as an expression reflecting our superstitious past. Although this may be only partly true during our period, it is interesting to observe that of the three original "greats" among psychiatrists—Adler, Freud, and Jung—he remains the main influence with more modern followers of psychiatry. Jung had by that time his thesis of the animus (male) and anima (female), which he presented as integral parts of the human psyche. The animus was the male portion of a female being, while the anima was the female quotient of a male. Jung always believed that his own anima helped him diagnose the troubles of his more difficult patients and inspired him with otherwise unobtainable information concerning the practice of his psychiatry. What most people would attribute to intuition or just lucky guesswork, he always ascribed to the work of his anima, and it is reputed that he gave her a very personal name that he never revealed in any of his writings.

The idea of each human having a bisexual nature with the physical qualities of one sex and the spiritual qualities of the other is a very old one indeed. Although Angels, or guardian spirits, were not supposed to be sexed at all, ancients frequently believed they were of the sex opposite to those humans they were supposed to protect. It was a common cultural custom to dress very young boys in girls' clothing or give them temporary "milk names" until they were due for fuller recognition as males. This practice was supposed to act as a prophylactic process against the malice of demons who meant to destroy humankind by wiping out its genetically weaker sex. Boy babies have always been recognized as being most difficult to rear until maturity, so they needed safeguarding by every device their mothers might think of. Hence the typically feminine ploy of deception or misdirection of unwanted attention by malignant spirits, which were frequently imagined as female in character.

Later this led to the belief in succubi, or female demons that derived their energy from the sexual potency of sleeping males, and in incubi, who obtained theirs from slumbering or fantasizing females. Erotic dreams resulting in emissions of seminal or vaginal fluids were believed to be the breeding grounds for fresh demons who would continue to torture their

human progenitors for eternities of existence. Mastur-
bating males were seriously supposed to father myriads
of fiends, which would all turn up to testify against him
at the famed Judgment Day when the final fate of
humanity would be decreed forever. Improbable as
this may sound, it is an example of deep-rooted beliefs
in the matching of human sexuality with a metaphysical opposite polarity.

A relatively recent exposition of such a theory can
be found in the "Compte de Gabalis" dating from the
late seventeenth century, in which the mating of humans
with elemental entities is discussed and dealt with
from a number of angles. For example, there is a state-
ment that Melchizedek was conceived in the ark by the
wife of Shem and a Sylph, or spirit of the air. There is
another reference to the enchanter Merlin being of extra-
mundane conception, having as parents a nun who
was the daughter of a British king, and a supernatural
lover who was also a Sylph. Virtually all of the first part
of the book is full of reputed instances concerning
humans being the result of superphysical pregnan-
cies. Though a great many of such stories could be
accounted for by unusual sexual fantasies, they still
serve as illustrations for the persistence of beliefs in
transsexual behavior.

A more modern exponent of bisexualism in human
beings was the German author Otto Weininger, who
in the early part of the twentieth century wrote a book
on the subject that appeared in English as *Sex and
Character*. His justifiable claim was that pure sex per se
was an undesirable quality, and that a beneficent blend
of both were needed to produce a pleasant and amiable

mortal. He postulated that if a 100 percent male could be imagined, he would be an absolute brute—powerful and pugnacious, not very bright, and dangerous to deal with—the ultimate macho type. His matching counterpart, the 100 percent female, could be described as a sort of super slut, cunning and nymphomaniac at the same time, exuding estrogen at every pore, and showing all possible signs of "cattiness" and associated antisocial behavior.

Such specimens of humanity, however, would be extremely rare, since we have become considerably modified by a judicious admixture of our opposite sex since our biological beings began. What Weininger was mostly concerned with was the precise percentage needed to produce a perfect balance between the sexes. In the end he took the physical sex as a baseline, and then calculated that if a human could exhibit 60 percent of that and 40 percent of its opposite, then the result would be an ideal individual. In other words there would be enough of the female in every male so as to create a gentler, more intelligent, and "softer" kind of creature, and enough of the male in every female to make her more outgoing, less devious, and a bolder or "harder" sort of soul. The defects of known male characteristics were to be improved by the inculcation of recognized female qualities and vice versa. Though the theory of this might seem sound enough, Weininger offered no suggestions of how such an ideal state might be brought about, apart from breeding suitably matched pairs until a consequent super race resulted. Such has long been the dream of those who hoped to establish a fresh paradise for their peoples on this Earth. Far from being a purely Germanic idea, it was foreseen by the Semites long ago. Hence their concerns with health and hygiene, plus their strict sexual codes and social customs.

The Hebrews in particular have always held as a basic belief that they are a chosen race, and must therefore preserve themselves as a unique section of humanity dedicated to whatever Deity may hold in store for them. This they have interpreted through their scriptures and traditions passed down amongst themselves and their affiliates for a multiplicity of generations. Being an extremely literate and versatile people, they have provided those outside their self-appointed limits with a means of studying and considering their findings from every possible viewpoint. Additionally, while laying down guidelines to their God concepts, they have also made available an intelligible ideology concerning a structural scheme of Creative Consciousness itself.

Many cultures in this world have legends concerning superior types of beings from other worlds who have made contact with ours and even interbred with humans, leaving bloodstock behind them that have been responsible for the whole of our progress and advancement as a species. It was they who made the difference between the apelike *Homo erectus* and the later *Homo sapiens*. In those times there was so marked a difference between ordinary Earth-bred creatures and the new "human-plus" people that these latter specimens almost automatically became the natural leaders and kings amongst their tribes of fellow beings. What is more, this has since been an ongoing process, and it is still continuing to this day, resulting in what we consider to be evolutionary advancement. Because in earlier times such a superior strain was limited to relatively few families, it became known as Blood Royal, later termed the Sangreal. Since that time it seems to have spread until becoming more or less common around the world, though naturally to varied extents and degrees of efficacy.

The Hebrews not only knew of this legend but wrote a version of it in the Book of Enoch, which is full of detail concerning names, functions, and even supposed happenings. Reading this book in modern times gives a very clear impression of an early visit by what we would now call a space mission of experts from another world much more advanced than ours who were trying to pass on some of their knowledge and experience to those of their kind on Earth. Apparently they managed to impart the rudiments of mathematics, astronomy, agriculture, and various crafts to their human pupils as well as interbreed with them until they either departed or died of natural causes. Of course to the pious Hebrews these visitors appeared to be wicked angels expelled from Heaven. To us, they seem more like a followup team subsequent to some previous and unrecorded mission that had accomplished the original implantation of a genetically viable bloodstock on Earth.

According to scriptural accounts there seems to have been more than just one visit to this planet by intelligent beings in ancient times. Witness the fiery chariot that swept Elijah up to Heaven in a whirlwind, and the stranger story of Moses obtaining instructions from his God on Mount Sinai. During that visitation God appeared only to Moses and eventually Aaron from behind a heavy smoke screen amid a great deal of noise from engines and amplifiers. Why would seventy selected elders eventually be allowed to view their God, under whose feet there would seem to be a sort of pavement like sapphire, and who "appeared as the body of heaven in his clearness" (Exodus 24:10).

To us, this seems like a projected image possibly of a holographic nature, but at the time it would have seemed an entirely supernatural happening. Why was it deemed necessary for the majority of Israelites present to wash themselves thoroughly and keep at a definite distance from the God-Moses trysting place, if not to avoid unwanted infections? What was any God doing with feet anyway? There are so many uncertainties if not very interesting possibilities concerning the written account of obtaining the Mosaic commandments, which were obviously a condensation from the forty known Egyptian ones of the period.

Yet despite this spectacular manifestation of their law-giving God, who seemed so obviously masculine, the Hebrews instinctively continued to honor their familiar female deities under the titles of Shekinah, Asherah, Anath, and later the Romanized description of the Matronit, probably a Semitic equivalent of the Magna Mater or Great Mother. It is impossible to eliminate all ideas of a Mother Goddess from the minds of those who have inherited her for many generations. One way or another she is going to express herself. With the Hebrews she remains personified as the Shekinah, who is considered to be the love aspect of God, and who is supposed to be in exile from Heaven until the total redemption of humankind, when she will reunite with the Eternal One forever. Meanwhile she continues to manifest the love and mercy of the Creator towards his chosen people of this planet.

Though the Hebrew concept of Deity may seem purely masculine, that is only nominally so, because strictly speaking it is seen as sex in action or in full congress with a willing partner. This is evident in the well-known saying, "God is love." The Hebrew word *AHB*, often *AHBH* but sounded *AH VAH*, means literally to "pant after," signifying the excited breathing of a pair inflamed by passion in the performance of a sexual coupling. In other words, it is a euphemism for an ideal sex act, implying the mating of both sexes in holy harmony with one another. Even the never-to-be-spoken Name of God, usually rendered *Yahweh*, is a two-syllabled word signifying a conjunction between the masculine Yah and the feminine Weh, almost in much the same way as we might write f_____ today, indicating that while everyone might know very well what the blanks represent, the word is treated as something that should not be uttered aloud but only apprehended privately by minds capable of coping with its full significance, which is of course the act of sex itself. Hebrews have always equated this ability as being one of divine importance.

It may be the male who initiates the act of generation by his injection of sperm, but it is always the female who is responsible for continuing the process not only until the moment of birth but also until the resultant human is technically able to care for itself. So we are much more our mothers' children than our fathers'. At earlier periods children stayed with their herds until they felt capable of fending for themselves in fresh territory. Their mothers showed them how to feed, while their fathers taught them how to fight and fornicate. They learned their needed skills for living from those around them, and although they were mostly concerned with discovering how to make the best use of their bodies, when these had been sensually satisfied they began to employ their minds as well, which is probably when the first notions of Deity began to dawn on them.

This at first would be a magnification of their Mother concepts into imaginary areas. Birth food and protection came from their mothers, so the non-material equivalents of such necessities must have been derived from the invisible images of those mothers they made with their own minds. That made good sense to them, so later they began to build up Father concepts that supplied the remainder of their requirements. Hence the association of God images with the fulfillment of human desires and requests. In other words, Gods and Goddesses were first seen in the light of Powers that answered, or appeared to answer, human prayers and specific petitions. As when children they had approached adults and often obtained what they asked for, so after they became adults themselves did they request from their Gods the equivalents of their needs and possibly demands. At that period the Gods recognized by most humans were simply highly magnified and idealized concepts of their own parents.

What they probably could not have realized was

that by mentally making such images and handing these down to their children genetically, they were focusing actual forces of nature into convenient forms of consciousness that could provide future power for the management of humankind's affairs at all levels of life. For instance, the clearer they could conceive a Mother-idea, and the better they could persuade their children to experience this for themselves, the more those children and their offspring in turn would be able to feel its meaning and express its qualities among those they shared their lives with. This would consequently enrich all the lives concerned with a Mother influence. The same was true in different ways with each type of Deity formulated. Sufficient attention paid to a war god or goddess would ultimately result in combat skills and weaponry expertise. Enough thought and activity devoted to a healing deity improved medical and surgical practice throughout the chain of consciousness activated. Our Gods became genuine reservoirs of approachable and employable energy.

Eventually it occurred to our most versatile minds that the best thing to do would be to conceptualize a kind of composite supreme God-Goddess able to exert total capability throughout all spheres of influence—a God that was omniscient, omnipotent, and omnipresent, hence approachable anywhere and knowing everything—in theory, an ideal sort of Being, although rather too remote and impersonal for the average human to handle comfortably. They might appreciate the practicality of such a concept, but most of them would feel happier dealing with one that came closer to their ideas of individual practice, which meant a specialist-

God for each particular requirement. In Pagan times this was perfectly possible, and in later Christian periods it was also made feasible by appointing some specific saint as the patron of whatever might be requested. While the actual energy needed to accomplish the prayer objective must necessarily come from Deity Itself, the techniques of applying that energy for such a particular purpose lay with the saint in question. As time went by, this saint-invoking practice became less and less popular, and increasing emphasis was laid on the efficacy of direct approach to the concept of Deity as an all-powerful authority capable of ordering whatsoever It will in this world or anywhere else, and so that seemed the most sensible and practical Power worth praying to.

However, such an approach, although presumed to be above all sexual implications, was derived from a basically masculine angle and adapted to a definitely masculinized Deity, whether considered as God the Father or God the Son. The originally feminine Holy Spirit had been neutered into a pure and indeterminate "Power" sometimes visualized as a dove, but otherwise seen as rays of light or individual flames. Exactly why all traces of official femininity had to be eliminated from the Christian conception of Godhood is rather puzzling, and the most elaborate evasions and improbable explanations have been put forward to cover the simple circumstances surrounding the so-called Virgin Birth, which was factually accomplished by artificial insemination. Sperm from selected "Godfathers" would be collected in a little horn with a small hole at its tip. This was inserted into the vagina of a dedicated temple virgin by an elderly woman who would also expel the seed by blowing down the open end of the horn. It would thus be perfectly true for the girl to afterwards disclaim all carnal contacts. Those concerned might indeed believe that Deity Itself had determined whose seed would win the race for the egg begetting the future child, and the whole operation could be considered as an immaculate act of a very sacred kind.

A clue connected with this is given in the Apocryphal Gospels, which mention that certain elders were told to bring their rods to the temple for inspection by the priests, and Joseph's was said to have brought forth a white blossom. One report told of a white dove flying from the end of it. It should not take much imagination to see that those were euphemized accounts of a fertility test for the erectability and satisfactory seed emission of proffered penises. Joseph obviously passed with honors, although it remains unclear if others were equally successful amongst the many evident failures. This might also explain the detailed genealogy of Jesus given in the Gospel of St. Luke as via the line of Joseph rather than of Mary his mother, which would have been more essential. Nevertheless, her reputed descent being from the House of David would automatically mean a direct relationship with the special Royal Blood flowing through the veins of all connected with it at that time.

What would have happened had Jesus proved female instead of male, and not died in Sacred King style as a political figure on a Roman cross but lived as a respected teacher-figure like Confucius, Lao-tse, or

Gautama Buddha, and whose words and example had inspired a following as great as theirs? Would there have been any such thing as Christianity today, and if not, then why not? Another question that needs to be asked is, What kind of feminine Deity concept might attract enough attention in our times to establish a fresh variety of faith that would endure to the extent of previous ones?

It could be pointed out that the spiritual systems advocated by Confucius, Lao-tse, and Gautama Buddha were not so much religions in a proper sense as they were ethical and moral codes of conduct. Jesus alone was promoted to God status by popular belief. It was not Gautama personally as a man who was represented by the images displayed in Buddhist temples, but the idea of *Buddhahood*, or *Attainment*. Despite endless theological arguments, it was the person of Jesus that was worshipped by Christians, mainly because of the miracles attributed to his physical presence before his death, and to his spiritual presence after it. Like Gautama, he was a human being who seemed to have achieved a state of divinity that proved it possible for others to do the same for themselves if they lived as he had shown them. He himself had said, "These things and greater shall you also do." Even so, it is doubtful if Christianity as such would ever have become a religion in its own right if those promoting it had not had the sense to adapt the best and most valued tenets of Paganism to Christianized frameworks and set this up for popular acceptance. So original Christianity was really reformed Paganism with strong overtones of Judaic morality. Since then it has been in a more or less continuing condition of reforming itself along increasingly restrictive lines, and probably has not yet reached its final focus. Nevertheless, it seems most significant that it has always been the human-divine status of Jesus Christ that remains the principal point of attention.

There have indeed been what might be termed "religoid" movements in modern times that originated from feminine sources. Although many minor ones may spring to mind, the most obvious are surely the Christian Science Church begun by Mary Baker Eddy, the Theosophical Society commenced by Helena Petrovna Blavatsky and Annie Besant, and the Spiritualist Movement beginning with the Fox sisters but promoted by a wave of women almost worldwide. All three associations have something in common: they are American in origin, and all are based on unusual or possibly out-of-the-ordinary factors. Christian Science began because of its mind-over-matter beliefs concerning bodily diseases, Theosophy because of its psychical and mystical beliefs deriving from Oriental philosophies and presumed "Masters" influencing human destinies from obscure Tibetan mountain retreats, and Spiritualism because of its claims to communicate with defunct people via mediums who were mostly women. None of the leading women concerned could have possibly claimed to offer themselves as Exemplar-figures or miracle workers of any kind, and yet the movements they began have not only survived but have attracted fairly large followings.

Early Christianity did not really prosper very widely until it officially commenced its cultus of the Holy Virgin Mother, who was really all the previous

Goddesses condensed into the persona of Mary, the mother of Jesus, and promoted to semi-divine status. Under such a classification she then became an object of what was termed hyperdulia. Reverence for holy or sacred Beings was deemed to be of three grades—the highest being divine, or that paid to the Supreme Being alone, and the lowest being *dulia*, or a type of reverence paid to saints or sanctified humans who had led holy or pious lives on Earth and were therefore entitled to attract the attentive thoughts and prayers from their fellow mortals after their deaths. Mary, however, was placed in a special class of her own by the official Church on account of her unique position, and was considered worthy of what became known as "hyper," or a grade above, dulia worship. In other words, she was recognized as a minor Goddess. Subsequently a large proportion of Christians refused to accept her privileged position, although they still allowed her sanctity while refusing to worship anything other than a masculine Deity. Stricter subsequent Christians denied the slightest sanctity to any human whatever, and only permitted prayers to be offered directly to that Deity Itself, which seemed to be becoming more and more masculine with every move in Its direction.

This state of affairs may have been tolerated while the majority of women tacitly accepted the dominance of the male sex in major fields of action such as wars, politics, finance, commercial enterprise, and similar other areas, but this scarcely applies to modern conditions in most civilized countries. Women are proving themselves not merely equal to, but frequently the superiors of, men, given comparable conditions of opportunity. In Nonconformist churches there have long been women ministers, and increasing pressure is being brought to bear on the established churches to allow the inclusion of women amongst their ordained ranks. These churches have always admitted, though very seldom encouraged, female deacons into their clerical grades, which is one degree lower than actual priesthood, entitling women in Holy Orders to officiate in any capacity except that of conducting the Eucharistic service. But women cannot become bishops or cardinals, although they could be canonesses, since the rank of canon means only a specialist in theological procedures or studies, and women have never been debarred from taking university degrees in theology. Women Doctors of Divinity are not all that uncommon, even though such might seldom satisfy an extremely ambitious or determined woman.

In olden times the function of female priestesses as servitors of some particular Goddess in temples dedicated especially to that Deity would have been entirely understood. Had the Christian Church declared as a doctrine that the Holy Spirit was the authentic feminine aspect of Deity and admitted a special order of priestesses to serve that particular spiritual principle, possibly in conjunction with the Virgin Mary as her human representative, things might have been vastly different today. As it is, the religious instincts of an increasing number of women are pressuring them internally to demand expression in ways that the official Christian Church neither approves of nor affords satisfactory outlets for. In ancient times it would have been a simple matter to offer themselves as accredited temple prostitutes, where they could presume themselves to be "Vessels of the Goddess" accepting the worship of males who saw themselves as mating with the Goddess during their act of copulation. Put into modern mystical terminology, those priestesses would be mediating the Goddess to her worshippers.

Pagans understood this concept very well, but Christians preferred to put it otherwise, although the wording, "with my body I thee worship" in the old form of marriage service is a survival of the older practice. Christians would only approve of sex within the blessed bonds of wedlock for the single purpose of begetting offspring, while Pagans saw it as an act of worship between a human male and the Goddess he was paying homage to. Children need not necessarily result from such a union, since the act itself would be devotional if intended in that way. Moreover, sex was by no means the only service proper for a priestess. Support for the sick and dying, comfort for the bereaved, counseling for the perplexed, instruction and guidance for children, and in fact whatever a woman could do best for her fellow mortals in the name of her Goddess would come within the scope of any truly dedicated priestess. That would be true today if such orders existed officially.

This is undoubtedly why so many women of our times are "opting out" of official Christianity in preference for Pagan pathways—adopting Goddess attitudes rather than isolating and amplifying the masculine principle of Deity alone into a position of supreme spiritual power. They are not demanding any sort of supremacy for themselves, but only their natural place as perpetuators of our race and species. It is true that one male can fertilize many females, but those females alone have the power to build up any resultant beings in their wombs and eventually send them out to join the rest of us. It is the women of this world that are the vessels who must bear the Blessed Blood amongst us if we are ever to gain the most Holy Grail of Godhood from this woeful world. Somehow we have to find an ideal concept to contain the Maid-Mother aspect of Deity we would all be willing to worship wholeheartedly. Perhaps if we look back a little towards the past we might perceive how it could be found to influence and benefit our future.

Eleusinian divinities:
Tripotolemus between Demeter and Kore

Chapter Two

*From Eleusis
to Epiclesis*

We might as well study the characteristics of the Mother-Mate Goddess at the peak of her popularity in Greece and Egypt, since both those civilizations are so well recorded and commented upon. Here we shall encounter her in the guise of Ceres-Demeter, the Greco-Roman Goddess, and Isis, her Egyptian counterpart. Both were noted for the purity of their worship and beneficience toward their human devotees. Their cults continued well past the Christian era until nearly the fifth century, and the likelihood is that they survived beyond that point in minor and less noticeable ways. Isis, who was equated with Athena as well as Ceres, was also the wife of her own brother Osiris. Egyptian royalty often wedded their siblings because of a belief that by doing so they were keeping their special royal blood in the family and thus safeguarding it. The mother of Isis was known under many names, possibly the most popular being Rhea or Ops, synonymous with Cybele, Bona Dea (Good Goddess), Magna Mater (Great Mother), and sometimes Athena. In fact it is wise to accept all the differently named Goddesses as all being aspects of the same feminine Deity, but looked at in different lights. For example, the aspect called Ops was derived from the Latin *opus*, which means "work," to show that she never gave anything without exacting effort to obtain it. She was represented as a matron with an outstretched right hand, as if to help supplicants, and loaf of bread in her left as if to remind people that they would have to work for their daily bread. Her husband was Chronus-Saturn, or Time and Experience. Both Isis and Ceres were agricultural Goddesses who taught their people how to look after their land properly and make the most of it. Since the time of Saturn and Ops was frequently referred to as the Golden Age, surely we can see here a lovely concept of a Mother-Goddess bringing a maximum of benefits to her human children, who believed in her enough to learn and work for what she and they both wanted.

Isis, her Egyptian counterpart, was another benefactress of her people, insofar as she instructed them in all the useful arts, especially the agricultural ones. Her story should be well known, and the murder of her husband by her brother-in-law Typhon, or Set, be remembered, after which she wandered throughout the land seeking his fragments, especially his missing genitals. This makes a beautiful fertility myth, recorded in the "Lamentations of Isis." Since Osiris is usually portrayed as being mummified and of a green color, bearing all the regalia of royalty, and Isis is shown as a living woman with an ankh in her hand, she may be considered as the Lady of Life, while he remains Lord of the Dead. As she was often shown in Mother form, holding the infant Horus in her arms, it is easy to see the origins of the familiar Madonna and child beloved by so many Christians at the present time. Maternity has always been a favorite archetype for humans, since it is evidence of a successful sex act, and therefore an encouraging justification for our continued existence.

As Ceres-Demeter, the Mother Goddess became the patron of the famous Eleusinian Mysteries, established in her honor in 1356 B.C. by Eumolpus at Eleusis in Attica. This festival was held every five years, and was open to both sexes of accredited good character and undoubted probity. No one guilty of witchcraft or any heinous crime was permitted to attend, and non-admission was tantamount to a character slur of the most serious kind. These mysteries were classified into two grades, the Lesser and the Greater, but nobody might be admitted to the Greater without first passing through the Lesser, which were celebrated at Agre near the Ilissus, a small river joining the sea at Piraeus. There they had to go through a purification by keeping themselves chaste for nine days, after which they were adorned with garlands while standing on the skin of an animal they had sacrified to Zeus-Jupiter, the Supreme God. Doubtless this was to remind them of the oldtime Sacred King sacrifices of chosen human beings on behalf of their tribes. After that they were entitled to call themselves *mystae*, or the initiated.

Not less than a year later they might apply for membership in the Greater Mysteries, which began by sacrificing a cow to Ceres, after which the secrets of the Mysteries were revealed to them under threat of fearsome oaths restraining them from betraying these. Promises of awful penalties were made, and those were taken so seriously that it was considered unlucky even to live in the same house as a betrayer. Candidates were first crowned with myrtle, and that had very special significance. The myrtle was first the tree of Venus-Aphrodite, and its boughs were also used to build the "booths" at the Hebrew Feast of Tabernacles. Its leaves were also the symbol of renewal, and were taken by the Greeks with them when they settled in new lands. Following the crowning, initiates were taken at night into the temple, where they were required to pass a number of trials and tests. They had to pass these successfully under pain of being rejected by the Hierophant conducting the ceremony. They had then to wash their hands in holy water and formally declare their innocence of intention. (Compare the Christian custom of placing a finger in holy water and making the sign of the cross over oneself before entering a Church.) Then the laws governing the conduct of initiated members were read to them from two stone tablets cemented together, called petroi. (Compare these with the Mosaic Tablets of the Law, or Commandments, which true Israelites must faithfully observe.) They were shown various tableaux and miming acts, which they were expected to interpret correctly, while every effort was made to frighten or confuse them. If they survived all those experiences successfully, they might emerge from the Greater Mysteries with the honorable title of *Epoptai*, or Inspectors, which was exactly the same as the Christian one of *episcopus*, or Bishop. Last of all, they were dismissed with the mysterious phrase, *konx ompax*.

Many attempts at interpreting this phrase have been made, but the most plausible option is probably "dust of Demeter" (or Ceres). This derives from *konis*, meaning "dust," and *Ompnia*, another title of Ceres. There could also be a connection with *omphe*, meaning "divine voice," or some token conveying divine intimations, or with the word *axones*, which were wooden tablets of the laws of Athens made to revolve around an axis. All these intimations would have the combined meaning of, "May we be reduced to dust if we do not obey the divine voice exhorting us to keep these laws." That would certainly make a lot of sense and meaning. Maybe, too, we might be reminded of the injunction, "Remember man, thou art but dust, and unto dust shalt thou return." It might also signify that corn grows from the dusty earth, which is the matrix from whence all material things are made and therefore represents the basics of being. Certainly *konx ompax* was taken to signify the crux of the entire ceremony.

The very garments worn by initiates during their ordeals were considered sacred and capable of warding off evils and enchantments, so they were normally worn until they almost fell apart, when they were either given to children or folded up and dedicated to the Goddess permanently. (Compare this with the Christian custom of creating relics from old garments of holy people.) In fact, everything to do with the Eleusinia, as these Mysteries were called, was considered sacred, and regular religious services appear to have been held with a priesthood consecrated for this purpose, of which the chief was the Hierophant, or

"Revealer of Sacred Things." The Hierophant had to be a citizen of Athens, and he held the office for life, although with the Celeans and the Philiasians it was for only four years. He was normally supposed to be single and chaste. To encourage such chastity obliged him to anoint himself regularly with hemlock, which was said to discourage sexual urges, as this bromide was reputed to do for the licentious soldiery of much later wars. The Hierophant was entitled to three principal attendants: a torch bearer, or *daduchos*, who was entitled to marry, a *kerux*, or herald, who acted as an announcer or crier, and a special supplicant whose duty it was to assist the Hierophant directly at the altar. (Compare these with the later Christian *acolyte, chorister*, and *deacon*, who were the principal assistants at the Eucharistic services.) In fact, a great deal of Christian practice and custom derives directly from the Eleusinian Mysteries held in honor of the Great Mother.

There were also other lesser officials to see that everything was ordered properly. The first of these was called the Basileus (or King), who was responsible for seeing that no indecency or irregularity took place, and under him there were four curators usually elected by the people. One of these would normally be from the Eumolpidae family, another from the Ceryces, and the remaining two from the ordinary citizens. There would be another ten people specially chosen to offer sacrifices at the festivals. Here we might be reminded of the ten members of a synagogue, or "minyan," who must constitute a minimum number of worshippers before any service may be considered valid therein. Christians later reduced this to two or three.

The quinquennial festival itself was always held in September, the Autumnal Equinox month, and normally from the fifteenth until the twenty-third so as to cover the date and time of the Equinox proper. During that period quite a number of local rules came into force. For instance, it would be illegal to present any petitions, or to arrest anyone under pain of a thousand drachmas fine, which would make $500 of our modern money; and if any woman rode into Eleusis by chariot she would be liable to a six-thousand drachma fine, or a bit more than $3000 today. This was to prevent too much distinction between rich and poor pilgrims, or at least to make this not quite so obvious. (Compare this with the clothing and jewelry regulations for Muslim pilgrims to Mecca for the same reasons.)

Initiated individuals had some special rules to observe. They were forbidden to sit on the cover of a well, or to eat beans, mullet, or weasels. Sitting on a well cover would place the posterior above drinking water, which would be an insult to the beneficent spirits believed to inhabit wells. One was not supposed to present one's posterior to anyone or anything considered sacred or respected. Since eating beans induced flatulence, one can see the practical reasons for discouraging this, but there was another significance too. Pythagoras had believed that beans derived from the same putrified matter from which humans had been formed at the beginning of the world, and therefore it would be impious to eat them. Also Demeter had given the Arcadians her permission to plant every pulse and grain except for the bean. Elections were sometimes held in those days by casting beans into a helmet, and so abstaining from beans signified avoiding political action. Seeing that mullet would be a major sacrificial fish during the festival, one can appreciate the reason for not eating this, but the flesh of weasels is by no means clear, except that those vermin have always been considered unwholesome. Additionally, since they represent elusiveness and treachery, those propensities would be highly undesirable amongst initiates of the Eleusinian order.

The first day would be spent as a social gathering called the Assembly, during which people simply got to know each other in friendly fashion, exchanging greetings and talking about matters of common interest. There was a great deal to be gained from this by no means pointless chitchat. It was a general easing into a spiritual situation that they intended to share together for the sake of experiencing a Concept they all agreed upon. Some may have attended several of these festivals, but there would always be those for whom it would be a first time, and the exchange of permissible information would have been most valuable and interesting for the newcomer. There must have been many attending for purely social reasons, or in the hopes of meeting those who might be of some advantage to them in business or similar areas, much as people belong to Masonic lodges or other ethical organizations in our times. However, this whole festival was ostensibly to honor the concept of a beneficent Being regarded as a Mother by all those present, so they would have to acknowledge this in some way, even if such was only formal and nominal.

The second day was spent mostly in the sea.

Though this was considered a ritual purification, it was significantly a return to our oldest mother in this world. How far the ancients realized this is very uncertain, but the instinct was certainly there. The Greeks in particular have always been a seafaring nation, but this intentional immersion in the ocean for ritual reasons is surely much more than a mere formality, being common to many cultures. With Christianity it has been reduced to baptism, but it has always been considered impossible to be a Christian until that rite has been performed. Hindus believe that bathing in Mother Ganges purifies them from all sins. Muslims are enjoined to cleanse themselves ceremoniously before entering a mosque, while Jews have their ritual baths at set intervals. Water and human worship are inseparable.

During the third day a solemn sacrifice of fish, which was supposed to be mullet, was made to Ceres-Demeter, together with some barley from a field cultivated for that particular purpose. This was considered to be so sacred that the priests themselves were not permitted to partake of it. Again we have a Christian connection, this time with the loaves and fishes that Jesus was said to have worked a miracle with by feeding a multitude with a minimum of bread and fish. There is also the symbol of the fish itself, one of the earliest symbols for Christ on account of the wordplay in Greek with his name. Plus, of course, his literal association with fisherfolk. The more such connections become apparent, the more likely it seems that early Christian practice was largely an extension of the ancient Eleusinia.

On the fourth day a procession was held in which the main object of attention was a consecrated cart bearing what was called the Holy Basket of Demeter. No one was ever told what, if anything, this contained, but it obviously represented the womb of our Great Mother and so was venerated accordingly. As it passed them, people greeted it with glad cries of "Hail Demeter!" Following this cart came women all carrying baskets in which were sesame, carded wool, salt, a serpent, reeds, pomegranates, ivy branches, and special cakes. All these items were of special feminine interest for those times. Both sesame and pomegranates were fertility emblems on account of their numerous seeds, and it was also supposed to be a pomegranate that Persephone, the daughter of Demeter, had eaten while crossing the Elysian fields, which prevented her permanent return to Earth. Wool was spun and woven by women to make clothing for their families, salt was used for preserving food, reeds for making baskets and some types of furniture, and the cakes had to be cooked with womanly skill. So far as the serpent was concerned, it was of the Aesculapian variety, and healing was very much a feminine art in its early days. Furthermore, if the serpent represented a living phallus, it could indicate sexual enjoyment without men, since those creatures were sometimes employed with their mouths sewn up for artificial sexual stimulation by insertion in women's vaginas. Occasionally live fish might be used for the same purpose, although these would not last so long as the serpent.

The fifth day was known as Torch Day, because at night everyone ran around with lighted torches in commemoration of Demeter lighting a torch from Mount Etna while searching for her lost daughter Persephone. People vied with each other in displaying the most impressive torches, and many accidental fires must have been started. Playing with fire is a very ancient practice, and it was always specially selected females who were appointed guardians of the Sacred Flame, which was never allowed to go out on pain of death. In very early times, responsibility for keeping a vital tribal fire alight was a very serious one indeed, for its extinguishment could mean ruin for many families. The Roman Vestal Virgins were descendants of those dedicated females, and the modern sanctuary lamps in Christian churches are current survivors.

The sixth day was known as that of Iacchus, who was taken to be the son of Demeter, and who accompanied his mother during her search for his sister and carried a torch in his hand to light her way during the dark periods. He also nourished her with a special drink composed of barley meal, grated cheese, and wine. (Do we have here a forerunner of the Christian sacramental meal?) His statue is shown as torchbearing, and is accompanied by myrtle-crowned followers. This torch was carried from Ceremicus to Eleusis with a good deal of banging on brazen vessels and dancing. By custom they rested at a place where a sacred fig tree grew. The cultivated fig is frequently fertilized by hanging strings of small wild fruit on it, and sexually suggestive rites accompanied this in early times, so we have the fertility motif again. The dancers also stopped at a bridge crossing the Cephessus, where they shouted derisory remarks at passers-by who, we presume, gave back as good as they got. After that they entered Eleusis by what was known as the mystical entrance. Here again we trace the mother and child theme, so common to most faiths, based in real antiquity: this time a quest for a missing daughter by her mother, supported by her brother, an enlightened son. Christians might note the "Light of the World" inference.

The seventh day was spent in sports and athletics, with prizes given to winning competitors, mostly consisting of generous measures of barley which might be used for brewing or baking. This cereal was reputedly first cultivated from its original wild grass at Eleusis, hence it had special significance. On the whole, this day would be considered one of relaxation and amusement, plus there was probably a great deal of gambling on the outcome of races and contests. Gatherings at Eleusis were meant to be both memorable and enjoyable, and sports were a certain way of ensuring that factor.

The eighth day was devoted to a repetition of the Lesser Mysteries, which afforded those who were not yet initiated an opportunity of experiencing them. This was said to have been because the famed Aesculapius, on his way from Epidaurus to Athens, had stopped at Eleusis in order to be initiated, and so it was felt that an equal opportunity should be opened for others in memory of that occasion. That could also account for the serpent in the earlier procession, which had become, and still is, the symbol of healing. The veritable Aesculapian serpent is a long, thin, and non-poisonous species of snake still common in Grecian rural areas.

The ninth and last day was termed that of the earthen vessels, because two large specimens of these were filled with wine and set up at the east and west of a specially dedicated place. After the necessary prayer formulae had been pronounced, both jars were simultaneously overturned and omens deduced from the way the wine flows met and mixed. In all probability there were marks and lines traced as a design on the earthen floor, and the pattern of the flows from either direction told the story for itself. One solitary ear of wheat was ceremonially reaped in complete silence, then very solemnly laid on the altar, after which the people were free to disperse quietly and go home at their own leisure, which usually meant some days later. They felt sure Demeter accompanied those she loved in spirit.

Such were the famed Eleusinian Mysteries, which were later taken to Rome during the reign of Adrian, who somewhat favored Christians; and most probably Christianity owes many of its original beliefs and customs to Eleusinian influence. We have always to remember, however, that the Mysteries owed their undoubted popularity and persistence entirely to the Maid-Mother concept they were expressly designed to honor. Not that they were by any means the only examples of their kind on Earth in those days, but at the time we are thinking of, the various Goddesses were mostly considered to be different aspects of the same One, each with some special spiritual function of her own. Nor might they all be totally good or evil, but inclined to either course as they pleased. This led to a lot of complicated speculations concerning the proper conditions for invoking the aid of specific Gods and Goddesses. Locations, times, and seasons were involved, as well as sometimes minute details concerning correct costume or symbology, which probably provided employment for those who specialized in such things. A lot depended on which light they were viewed by.

For instance, the Goddess Hecate, once held up as a horrid example of evil, would never have been seen as such by her original devotees any more than Kali would be considered in that way by modern Hindus. Hecate was certainly a Goddess of spells and enchantments, but she was the Deity appealed to for protection against their malignancy. She had several spheres of influence, being a triple Goddess known as Diana of the Crossroads, since she was seen in triplicate as the Lunar Goddess Diana in the heavens, Hecate on Earth, and Persephone in Hades below. She was said to have three faces, those of a mare, a bitch, and a sow—all sacrifical animals. Those were of course the three phases of the Moon, and she was reputed to have a fourth face that none might see and stay alive, since the dark side of the Moon was supposed to offer a home for departed spirits. Hecate was the special patron of childbirth, and the feminine equivalent of Plutus, God of wealth, because she produced wealth and prosperity for realms and their rulers. Her proper sacrifices were dogs, lambs, and honey, and they were usually made at a crossroads because of her name Trivia (Threeways).

At Athens in particular, well-to-do citizens would arrange a supper to be laid out at a road junction every New Moon in honor of Hecate, and then would call on her loudly three times afterwards, departing without ever looking backwards. Poor and hungry people would then emerge from concealment and devour the feast, which it became a polite fiction to assume that Hecate had eaten herself. As an excuse for offering charity without offending the pride of the poor, Hecate must have been a much-worshipped Goddess, even though being given a very much undeserved reputation for witchcraft by later Christians. Also associated with the Moon was Artemis, who was said to be an alter ego of Hecate's. She was greatly addicted to chastity, besides being a militant supporter of what we would now call feminism. She had a permanent bodyguard of females from the Oceanides class, or sea nymphs, who had all taken vows of perpetual celibacy.

A connected aspect of Persephone was Libertina, who presided over funerals, because death donated freedom from the last of bodily ills on Earth. She had a temple in Rome that kept a death register for the payment of a small fee, and as Libertas, she was usually depicted as a young woman with a rod in one hand and a cap of freedom in the other. The rod was used by whichever magistrate presided over the manumission ceremony, which entitled her to wear the cap. Sometimes she was shown with a cat at her feet, since the independence of that animal was well recognized in the ancient world. Another form of this Goddess was Libentina, to whom nubile young women dedicated all their childish toys as a sign of freedom from childhood and acknowledgment of their readiness to assume adult responsibilities as wives and mothers. The toys would later be given to less privileged children. This was the custom mentioned by St. Paul when he spoke of "putting away the things of a child."

One of the best-known aspects of the Goddess was that of the Bona Dea or the Magna Mater. This was served purely by respectable matrons much along the lines of a women's Masonic lodge. Their Goddess was reputed to be so chaste that no male except her husband ever saw her, and at meetings for her worship, any statues of male personages were covered with cloth and no male was allowed entrance. Eventually, however, inquisitive males wearing wigs and feminine attire managed to attend some of these gatherings and reported them as being lewd and obscene almost beyond belief. Though we are not told exactly what such lewdness consisted of, we might make a good guess at cunnilingus, use of artificial phalli, and similar sexual stimulations to the point of orgasm. There must have been considerable deterioration of these Magna Mater gatherings over the course of time, since the original titles of Good Goddess and Great Mother do not suggest gross indecency of any kind. Moreover they did not admit juveniles, as some other cults allowed.

Yet there actually was a specialized Goddess of sexual license called Cottyto, whose rites were reported to be so disgusting they even offended the Goddess herself. Her priests were called Baptae, because they would wash themselves in what was described as an offensively feminine manner. Meetings of this curious cult always took place at night. Sometimes the devotees would carry branches of trees decorated with sweets or trinkets which anyone was entitled to pick if they wanted to. This is an early example of a Christmas tree, showing clear Pagan origins. The poet Eumolpus (c. 440 B.C.) parodied the priesthood of this cult so bitterly in his comedy "The Baptae" that the priests are said to have arranged his murder, and anyone who revealed exactly what happened at their secret gatherings might expect to be killed. They were obviously not a very nice lot. Cottyto, however, was presumed to be the "naughty" side of Persephone. As Queen of Hades, there was a belief that before anyone could die, Persephone or her colleague Atropos, the lethal one of the Three Fates, had to remove a single hair from their heads. Hence arose the custom of cutting hair from a deceased person's head and offering it to Persephone by strewing it on the ground outside the house. Persephone, it will be remembered, was half-sister to Plutus, the God of wealth, who was shown as being blind because he distributed wealth so indiscriminately, and lame because it came so slowly, yet with wings to show how fast it could all fly away again.

All these characteristics and attributes are illustrations of how human beings imagined their directive Deities in days long gone by. Have we replaced them with any better examples, or are we doing no more than letting them drift into useless obsolescence? Perhaps even worse, are we making far more dangerous and damaging creations of consciousness from what we fear or dread yet realize perfectly well are the most vicious propensities of our natures? There is one archetypal Mother that most of us would acknowledge to some extent, to wit, Mother Nature herself; but how do we visualize or condense her within our consciousness? In other words, what would be the best way of evoking her into contemporary awareness so that she would become an intensely active and individual inspiritment for anyone seeking spiritual liberation and enlightenment?

Why should we seek a matriarchal principle of Deity anyway? No one should seek such a thing exclusively of its male counterpart, but we have already sought to exclude the feminine element of God for so many centuries that we have become unbalanced; and we now need to reestablish the equilibrium of energy by mating the polarities of Power with each other so as to cause a state of Cosmos between both conditions of spiritual being. In the old days we would have said that no male God could possibly be complete without its correct counterpart in order to create a perfect Power. Matching all our Deity concepts in ourselves would amount to the ideal "mystical marriage," which is advocated as the ultimate aim of every esoterically minded individual.

For example, if we sought to become ideal Christians, we should see the sexual connection between a Father ideal, a Mother ideal, and a resultant Son or Daughter ideal: God the Father, God the Mother, and God the Issue. That could become possible if the now neutral Holy Spirit were restored officially or by personal belief to its original feminine gender. This is actually implied in the Nicene Creed when it is stated that Jesus "came down from heaven and was incarnated by the Holy Spirit out of the Virgin Mary and was made human." In other words Mary was deputizing for the Holy Spirit, whom God the Father had duly mated with, making a spiritual offspring that could only become human if it found a willing womb capable of materializing it. Thus the spiritual mother of Jesus was the Holy Spirit, while Mary, spouse of Joseph, supplied his physical body only. For Christians who are able to arrange their thinking along those lines, there should be no difficulty in coming to terms with their faith in the most mystical way.

Such was in fact the secret of the Holy Grail cultus, which firmly maintained that the consecration of the sacred elements of bread and wine in the Eucharistic Liturgy was invalid because it did not employ what were described as the "extra efficacious words." The actual words themselves were never disclosed in plain language, although they were entrusted to "Keepers of the Grail," none of whom were believed to die happily unless they had passed the formula down to some trusted confidant.

What do we actually know about those words? Very little, yet what is known happens to be most significant. We are told that Joseph of Arimathaea, reputed to be the Virgin Mary's uncle, received them from Jesus personally, and they were "tender and precious, gracious and compassionate." Elsewhere the mysterious words were translated as "sweet, gracious, precious, and piteous." Such a close description of their meaning could scarcely have been written without a reasonable knowledge of the words themselves. There was obviously something about their quality that evoked ideas of gentleness, great value, and fellow-feeling combined with sympathetic love in the mind of their evaluator. What type of words would be most likely to do that? About the first point that stands out before all others is that collectively they seem notably feminine in character rather than masculine. That is to say, it is as though Jesus were speaking of something or someone of a feminine nature that he valued or loved greatly, and that he would wish to be likewise honored by others who might appreciate this also. So just who or what would Jesus be likely to speak of in such a fashion?

The answer to this can only be whatever represented to him the feminine aspect of Deity—perhaps the personal name of his own mother, Miriam, whose name means the ocean, reputed to be the original mother of all living creatures on this planet, or a Goddess-name like that of the Shekinah, said to be a feminized presence of God as the Ecclesia of Israel. Again, Jesus could have been acknowledging his own feminine characteristics or even a combination of all these factors. Whatever precise terms Jesus may have used are beside the point here; the important issue at stake is their feminine significance. Once this is clearly understood and agreed with, we can attempt to replicate the formula itself in quite a number of ways. It is the recognition of the principle involved that is of primal importance.

The Grail itself has been defined as a sacred vessel said to have been used by Jesus to contain the wine he consecrated as his own blood and shared with his intimate disciples at the famous Last Supper. Since that time it has been physically lost to this world, yet it remains as a source of inspiration for those who hope to attain a spiritual goal in life. Such souls are supposed to be those of good breeding who are prepared to spend their lives in such attainment. Thus the Grail is taken as a supreme incentive in spiritual spheres, and has now become virtually synonymous with any long-sought objective of maximum importance to its seeker.

There is a great deal of Grail literature in existence, though the exact nature of the Grail itself is never clearly defined or described beyond all possibility of doubt. Everything is always hinted at, alluded to, or otherwise indirectly dealt with. Nevertheless, when its entirety is taken as a meaningful movement within the Christian Church as a whole, an overall intention of restoring the proper place of a feminine aspect to its Godhead becomes evident. Women were always described as "vessels," and some of the Virgin Mary's proudest titles are Spiritual Vessel, Honorable Vessel, and Singular Vessel of devotion. Virtually all the legends connected with the Grail leave those familiar with it in no doubt of its feminine significance: the female Vessel assumed to be a Cup, yet always connected with a bleeding and masculine Spear denoting Royal Blood or a line of descent from sacred sources continuing through a maternal factor.

In the earliest versions of the Mass or Christian liturgy, when it came to the crux of the consecration itself, distinct mention was made of the feminine aspect of Deity as the Holy Spirit, but later on with the Western or Roman style, this was removed altogether so that a purely masculine implication remained. The Eastern Orthodox Church, however, retained this Holy Spirit clause in its consecration formula and still uses it to this very day, which seems to substantiate the probability that the originators and propagators of the Grail cultus were those who believed in and loved the idea of a feminine Deity principle, and subsequently were trying to restore it to what was indeed the most important point of their liturgy.

The early Christian Church had four main liturgies: the Eastern, the Alexandrian, the Roman, and the Gallican. It was a version of the Gallican that was first used by the Celtic Church until eventually being replaced by the Roman Rite subsequent to St. Augustine of the seventh century. The original Gallican liturgy was reputedly written by St. John especially for the Church at Ephesus, a city that was renowned for the worship of the Goddess Diana. It was introduced into Gaul by Irenaeus when he became bishop of Lyons in A.D. 177. The Johannine Gospel, which was the only one accepted by the Cathar sect, makes no mention of the bread-wine incident at the Last Supper, but does record the remarks of Jesus concerning the mysterious "comfortor" Spirit he would send in his place. It is also the only Gospel that mentions the spear piercing the side of the crucified Jesus, and Nathaniel calling him the Son of God and King of Israel.

Since the Mozarabic version of the Gallican liturgy developed under the Visigoths in Spain lasted the longest and carried the Holy Spirit clause, this may have been the one which Grail cultists had mostly in mind. The consecration formula went, "Truly holy, truly blessed is your Son Jesus Christ our Lord, in whose name we offer to you Lord these holy offerings, praying that you will be pleased to accept and bless them by the outpouring of thy Holy Spirit," etc. The Mozarabic liturgy and chant system is still kept up in one Cathedral alone, Toledo, which has practically become a church within a Church.

A very early Coptic version of the consecration formula puts it: "We make the remembrance of his death, offering to you your creatures this bread and this cup. We pray and beseech you to send out over them your Holy Spirit, the Paraclete from Heaven, to make this bread the body of Christ, and the cup the blood of Christ of the new covenant," etc. An Alexandrian liturgy of St. Mark (c. 450 A.D.) is a lot more detailed and explicit when the consecratory prayer implores the Lord God to "send out from your holy height, from your prepared dwelling place, from your unbounded bosom, the Paraclete Itself, the Holy Spirit of Truth, the Lord, the Lifegiver, who spoke through the Law the prophets and the apostles, who is present everywhere, and fills everything, who on Its own authority and not as a servant works sanctification on whom It wills in your good pleasure; single in nature, multiple in action, the fountain of divine endowments, consubstantial with you, proceeding from you, sharing the throne of the Kingdom with you and your only begotten Son our Lord and God and Savior Jesus Christ, look upon us and send upon these loaves and these cups your Holy Spirit to sanctify and consecrate them as Almighty God, and make this bread the body and these cups the blood of the new covenant of our Lord and God, Savior and King of all, Jesus Christ."

The Eastern Orthodox Church, which had left the original formula intact with its liturgy of St. Basil, said at its crucial point: "We represent to thee these figures of the holy body and blood of thy Christ, and beseech thee O thou Holy of Holies that thou wouldst be graciously pleased that thy Holy Spirit may come upon us and upon these gifts set forth to bless, hallow, and declare this bread indeed the precious body of our Lord and God and Savior Jesus Christ, Amen." The priest then goes on to pray for the Christian Church while the following hymn is sung in honor of the Virgin Mother of Jesus on Earth: "O full of grace thou art the joy of all creation, of the assembly of angels and the race of men; thou hallowed Temple, spiritual paradise and boast of maidenhood, whence God took flesh when he was before the worlds our God became a child. Thy womb he made his throne, and he enlarged thy bosom broader than the heavens. O full of grace thou art the joy of all creation. Glory be to thee."

The retention of this Holy Spirit clause was known as the *epiclesis*, or "extra efficacious words," and they or their equivalents were reputed to be those missing from the Mass as claimed by those of the Grail cultus. It is perhaps interesting to note that two of the terms, "precious" for the body and blood of Christ, and "gracious" for the Virgin Mary, are those used in describing the secret of the Holy Grail. It should also be noted that a third term, "tender," is often employed with reference to very young children, which was certainly a relationship Jesus shared with Mary once.

Although the Roman and Western liturgy mentioned both the Holy Spirit and Mary the Mother of Jesus in many other places, the feminine principle remained absent from the actual consecratory formula, and it was at this especial focal point where the Holy Grail cultists felt it most necessary to be openly and plainly acknowledged as a coequal partner in the production of Jesus as a personified and humanized Deity. After all, the scriptures they believed in and tried to follow as best they could had distinctly said in Genesis 1:27: "So God created man in his own image. In the image of God created he him, male and female created he them." In the image of God created he him, male and female created he them." Therefore if man was a biological being, then so was God if scriptures were true, which in those days people believed them to be. Moreover, the next verse of Genesis went on to say: "And God blessed them and said unto them, be fruitful and replenish the earth and subdue it, and have dominion over the fish of the sea and the fowl of the air and over every living thing that moveth upon the earth." This was plainly a Creator who encouraged fertility and sexual reproduction, or union between males and females.

It may seem a little strange to moderns that early Grail cultists should be so persistent and particular on the point of including a feminine potency in the consecratory formula of consumable elements believed to not only represent but actually *become* the body and blood of their Savior God Jesus. However, we must remember that the entire division between the Eastern and Western Churches took place when the former officially denied the proposition of the Holy Spirit proceeding equally from the Father and Son of the Holy Trinity, as Rome opined. The Pope at that time promptly excommunicated all Eastern Christians, and the Patriarch of Constantinople retaliated by repudiating the followers of the Western and Roman Church. Seemingly the Eastern view was that the Holy Spirit derived directly from the Father, and the Son was a result of these two Principles mating—in other words, a straightforward Father-Mother-Child relationship so comprehensible and acceptable to early Christians, who were quite accustomed to Goddess concepts and ideas of sexual relationships between Divine Beings.

It should be self-evident that the neutralization of the hitherto feminine aspect of Deity in the Western Christian Church would be very upsetting to those who loved and wanted her as a worship-objective. Therefore they would naturally band together under some mutually uniting symbol they could all agree upon and understand exactly what it stood for. What better choice for such a sign than the Blood of Christ itself for several special reasons. First of course because they regard this as the seal of their own salvation, but perhaps more importantly, because among the ancients it was always considered that a man derived his blood lineage through his mother. For that reason, when a circumcision was performed, a drop of the infant's blood was taken up by a finger of the officiating *mohel*, stirred into some wine in a kiddush cup, and offered to the mother first in acknowledgment of what was rightfully hers. After that the presumed father and the rest of the family partook in turn.

In the case of Jesus, that Cup of Blessing signified not only his Earthly mother Mary but also his Heavenly Mother the Holy Spirit. By selecting the sacred Vessel as their special symbol and terming it the Holy Grail,

Sangreal, or Blood Royal, its adopters felt that they were choosing the essentially feminine part of the sacrament which they hoped and intended to replace where it properly belonged. As they saw it, the bread that represented the flesh of Jesus corresponded with the male part of the sacrament for this reason. When the *mohel*, or circumcising rabbi, neatly removed the male baby's tiny foreskin, he usually disposed of this morsel by swallowing it himself, thus keeping it part and parcel of the Hebrew tradition and essentially male. So when Jesus instituted his memorial meal, with bread symbolizing his flesh and wine his blood, many saw this as a bisexual sacrament with bread representing his masculinity, while wine typified the purely feminine side of his nature. Therefore to partake of the sacrament properly and wholeheartedly, each element should be consecrated according to its significance and accepted in the same manner.

This means to say that in the view of those subscribing to the Sangreal Concept and upholding the Holy Grail ideology, the compleat and correct Christian sacrament would be a unified twofold affair presenting their God as It really is, being an image of themselves as a bisexual entity: bread symbolizing the male, and wine the female quotient of the God Who or Which was entering them as saved souls. Such was, and for that matter still is, the inmost secret of the Holy Grail. It should be specially noted that the cult was especially Western and virtually unknown in realms where the Eastern Orthodox Church predominated. So it was probably small wonder that the Roman Church eventually declared the cult of the Holy Grail heretical, although only in a doctrinal sense, which meant it could continue as a topic of art, poetry, or literature providing it was confined to romantic mythology and never promulgated as a serious religious dogma.

Hence the Sangreal Concept in its Christian form remained and thrived in that condition for centuries, while Christianity on the whole remained a male-dominated religion, even though women were always its principal supporters and propagators, to say nothing of its saints and martyrs. However much the Church may have preached or encouraged the theory of male-female equality, it certainly did not permit such a thing in practice. Nor did it ever alter its consecratory formula with the entirely male implications. Even though most intelligent moderns know perfectly well that normal humans are a blend of both male and female natures, and that therefore Jesus must have had his due quotient of Femininity, it would still make a welcome gesture to acknowledge this fact somehow in official Christian liturgies as it has already done elsewhere.

It was not until the seventh to ninth centuries that the Roman rite ceased communicating the sacrament in both kinds to the laity, due to what they considered the "barbarous habits" of those people. It was mostly the sight of the sanctified wine on the beards of the men, often wiped off carelessly with the back of a hand, that gave most offense. This did not happen with the clean-shaven Roman clergy; the Eastern Orthodox Church, whose priests and monks were customarily bearded, dealt with the same problem by providing a silver tube through which communicants could suck their share of wine from the chalice, or sometimes a spoon was used for placing the wine directly in opened mouths. Occasionally partakers were permitted to dip a small portion of their bread in the sanctified wine, thus obtaining the required togetherness.

The argument adopted by the Roman Church, however, was that whereas blood could always be separated from flesh and dispensed by itself, flesh would always contain traces of blood. Therefore the bread alone, which signified the flesh of Jesus, should theoretically suffice as an adequate sacrament truly representative of the total Christ. Lay supporters of the Holy Grail cultus, however, felt that they had most unfairly been deprived of their sacred symbolism. What they were being told to accept seemed to them nothing like the full male and female quotients of Deity on equal terms with Itself, but only whatever female qualities might exist in a masculine God when separated from his rightful mate. Thus to such people in particular, it would appear like a very second-rate or substitute sacrament.

Nevertheless, the cult of the Virgin Mother was growing in popularity with all sorts of pious practices, such as the Rosary, the Litanies and Novenas, and the Angelus. The name of Mary was being coupled with that of Jesus by Christians throughout Europe, and memorials of this were appearing in unexpected places. At the then newly erected Lady Chapel of the rebuilt Glastonbury Abbey, which has always had Holy Grail associations, there is still to be seen a stone at eye-level height to the right of the south door exterior, with two names inscribed in five-inch letters:

IESVS
MARIA

Another notable place where the same words appear was on the blade of a sword borne by Joan of Arc, the hiding place of which was revealed to her in a vision. It was supposed to be the sword of Charles Martel, the grandfather of Charlemagne, who in A.D. 732 managed to stop the Saracen invasion of Europe, thus assuring the future of its Christianity. JESVS–MARIA were also the words embroidered on Joan's famous banner, which she carried everywhere, and she possessed a ring with the same inscription. Was this device a special code whereby devotees of the Holy Grail were known to each other? It is tempting to suppose so. If there could be the slightest possibility of this, we might easily believe that Jesus passed on the secret of the Sangreal with words which signified: "I and my father are one by Faith, but my Mother and I are one by Blood. Hallow us both by a belief binding us together by living LOVE."

According to the Gospel of John, the first public wonder-working act of Jesus was at the instigation of his mother, when she cajoled him into causing plain water to seem like the most expensive wine at a wedding feast they were attending together at Cana. There have even been speculations that this wedding might have been his own, although there is no supportive evidence elsewhere. Still, it could be mystically significant that wine was associated with the beginning and end of his Messianic career. In fact, the vital "extra efficacious words" guarded by so many generations of faithful Keepers of the Sangreal Secret may well have been something like: *Hallowed be this bread that manifests the male, and this the wine which means the fertile female form of our own Ladylord of life, creating and preserving all through perfect love. Blessed be my holiest name Iesu Mari, amen.*

The names here, of course, to be taken not so much as those of Jesus and his mother personally, but as being representative of an idealized humano-divine Being who personifies the very best and finest all our human race can ever become. Or literally, the fulfilled Quest of the Holy Grail itself.

We have seen how civilized people of olden times considered their Goddess figures as beneficent beings intending only the best for their faithful followers. What might she appear like dressed in our customary clothing and behaving in accordance with the best of our beliefs and ideology, or the finest of our feminine ideals magnified to Godsize? She would be as always a perfect mother, mate, mistress, sister, and female friend, all combined as one. Males might certainly make her their ideal sex partner, and although some women could see her in that same light, they could also appreciate her in common with the men as mother, sister, and friend, or even daughter: a supreme figure of their own sex, who would understand and sympathize with them completely, offering all possible support during all the difficulties of their lives; someone entirely sensible of what everything means to them—their misgivings, hopes, and problems of every description— to sum her up, a perfect person of their own kind.

Perhaps since the Sangreal concept came so close

to this idea in previous periods, we might as well adapt it to our times under the novel title of our Blessed Bloodbeing, and see how that can be fitted into contemporary frameworks. Since blood is common to both males and females, its only difference being in regard to type, such a title would apply to either gender and could be appropriate as a cover-concept for whichever aspect or polarity might be required. Such would certainly be in accordance with our oldest and most sacred beliefs in blood per se, when it was taken to be the actual life of every creature and was considered to be a proper sacrifice to any deity whatsoever, whether literally or symbolically. Christians still speak of being "washed in the blood of the lamb" (such an animal being the acceptable sacrifice made by an average Jewish family at their temple), and it has always been the blood sacrifice of Jesus' own body that was believed to have redeemed the whole world from its sins. If we can accept the symbology of blood as being synonymous with our salvation in any sense, we may surely see it as representing whichever aspect of Deity we intend to relate ourselves with. To this day we believe that blood relationship constitutes the closest ties between humans, and if we need still closer connections with the best of our spiritual beliefs, then the spiritual equivalent of blood ought to be our ideal representation.

Chapter Three

The Blood Beginnings

As every instructed schoolchild should know, the first sign of pregnancy or anticipated motherhood is the cessation of the normal female blood flow. This is because all the blood will be needed for building up a fetal body inside the womb. We are truly begun with blood in its literal sense, and the slight effusion of blood that indicates the initial penetration of the hymen and the consequent end of technical virginity was always regarded as a sacrificial sign. Many rural Middle Eastern mothers are still supposed to exhibit bloodstains on the sheets of their sons' bridal beds to prove both the virginity of their new daughters-in-law and the virility of their sons. Most of the witnesses present outside the house or bridal chamber know perfectly well that the blood will almost certainly have come from a dove or pigeon, but the show is expected to please everyone. The symbol of a dove should be carefully noted by those seeking signs of the feminine Holy Spirit, since the dovelike Holy Spirit would symbolize the shedding of blood by the Virgin Mary when her hymen was presumably penetrated by God the Father in the shape of a human, sperm-filled horn wielded by an old woman.

Probably before, but certainly during, the Middle Ages, the first official coupling of a royal pair was scarcely considered proper unless blessed by a bishop. Such an ecclesiastical dignitary was expected to bless the royal couple in bed together, invoking God's gift of fertility upon them with holy water to symbolize the flood of sperm it was hoped would proceed from the regal penis in order to produce an authentic heir from the queenly womb awaiting it. Whether bishops were supposed to witness the sexual act itself or not is somewhat uncertain, but they were positively required to be present at least in some adjoining room during a royal birth. This was to ensure the immediate baptism of an infant should that prove necessary. The Church had by that time recognized the validity of baptism in utero if impractical otherwise. This called for inserting a syringe filled with holy water into the mother's vagina and squirting this onto the head of a tardily arriving child while uttering the short formula confirming the infant's Christianity. Whether that could be considered really valid in the case of a breech presentation is a moot point. It was a seldom-used practice, however, and it was supposed to prevent the passage of an unbaptized soul into the hypothetical Limbo, where it would await some ultimate divine decision.

Considered as a vital fluid capable of causing all sorts of wonders and even miracles, blood has always excited and inspired humans with unusual thoughts and feelings. It was so closely associated with birth and death that it presented a maximal meaning between these two ends of a lifetime. At one time a condemned noble person was granted a noble death by effusion of blood, which would at least afford a privileged exit for his soul through its flow, while a commoner could expect an execution by strangling, which only allowed the soul a bodily exit by way of the anus, and so one would suffer shame and disgrace in consequence. Heretics had to be burned, of course, so as to avoid the shedding of blood, which might be collected and used as a relic. Although churchmen were prohibited from deliberately shedding blood, bishops partaking in actual battle were allowed to fight with maces only, which were assumed to cripple an opponent by concussion alone, possibly without killing him, and so avoiding outright murder.

The significance of blood throughout our history has been profound, and it has often been associated with spectacular healings. A classical cure for epilepsy once was to drink the blood of newly slain gladiators, which was also supposed to revitalize weakened bodies. In fact the main reason that old Roman arenas were so well patronized was that people hoped to see fit and healthy men reduced to bloody carrion. Despite what anyone may claim, the fundamental reason why dangerous sports are so popular today is that it is subconsciously hoped that some fatal accident might occur, with consequent bloodshed thrilling onlookers with delicious horror. Public executions have always been popular, and if these were revived in our times with sales of expensive tickets for the best seats, there would probably be enough money raised to pay off all the national debts in existence. The overwhelming popularity of football is undoubtedly due to an instinctive sense of the game's descent from the custom of kicking the severed heads of enemies around after a battle. The head of Cromwell's corpse, when exhumed for ceremonial execution after the Restoration, was kicked around the streets of London before being spiked on Temple Bar, and it eventually passed into private possession for a considerable period before being buried in the grounds of his old Cambridge college.

Blood was also used for compounding many witchcraft specifics connected with cursing and evil-wishing, validating documents consigning souls to the Devil in exchange for seven years of his faithful service, and many similar practices. To the contrary, be it noted that the meaning of the English word "blessing" derives from *bledsian*, or holy blood (Sangreal again), signifying the blood-drops from a sacrifice upon an altar being scattered with special bunches of twigs over the heads of a gathered congregation. It was generally believed that even a single drop would be efficacious in bringing good fortune and favors to whomsoever it touched. Hence the beneficent intentions implied by bidding blessings on anyone. Today the scattering of lustral water takes the place of the more ancient blood-drops, even when the intentions are much the same.

It may be interesting to bear in mind the claims of modern radiesthesists that they can diagnose and treat any form of disease through a single drop of blood taken from a living being, whether animal or human. There was a certain amount of scandal respecting the authenticity of such modified "Abrahams Boxes" offered for purchase some years ago. People were paying good money to the practitioners who were operating those machines, just as their ancestors were doing to reputed wonderworkers of their times for casting spells and constructing talismans. Modern mortals are no different when they attempt to buy blessings from electronic gadgets of impressive appearance that make unsubstantiated claims for success. Nevertheless, these dubious machines did demonstrate something very definitely; a surviving belief in blood itself as an agent of human intentions. If blood acted as a focus for faith alone, that could accomplish a great deal of good— or harm.

Again it might be remembered that the red color of blood played, and still plays, an important part in our lives. It was an ancient sign for sex in Rome, where official whores had to wear red head scarves to indicate their profession, and brothel areas anywhere are still known as "red light" districts. There is also a common expression in English, "red hat = no drawers," which is obviously of very old origins. Early chieftains in Rome used to paint their bodies red in preparation for war, partly to honor Mars and hopefully to scare the enemy, but mostly to prevent panic on their own side if they saw their chiefs bleeding badly. This later became the reason for red coats on British officers. Red light is much used among color therapists for energizing feeble patients, because it is thought to stimulate the blood corpuscles. Because it is suggestive of blood, red is almost universally recognized as a signal for danger.

On the familiar figure of the Tree of Life glyph too,

red is the central sign of Severity in the middle of the feminine Black Pillar on the left facing an observer. Being a male-dominated culture, the Hebrews would naturally associate the least-liked human characteristics with the female sex, and yet this particular quality is a vital one. It signifies severity in the sense of law and order, or whatever means of ensuring good behavior. Here we can see the maternal equivalent of controlling the conduct of troublesome offspring by judicious retribution. There is not the slightest hint of cruelty or injustice implied by this Severity concept. All it should signify is the common-sense control of bad behavior by any practical means called for. From a cosmic viewpoint this might be taken as karma, or the requital of wrongs by divine retribution, which might be expected by any reasonable person, especially from a Mother-Goddess reproving her human children.

The worst sort of mothers are those who make not the slightest attempt to control their children's conduct or guide them in any direction. Such children will naturally grow up with their worst characteristics dominating their behavior, not only spoiling their own lives but also those of others unfortunate enough to come into close contact with them. Being an ideal mother who knows how to administer discipline with just the needed degree of severity tempered by love and care for her children's well-being is probably one of the most difficult duties that any human being is ever expected to fulfill. People finding such mothers in the flesh are very fortunate, but there is nothing to prevent others from seeking her in the Spirit if they feel so inclined. That is precisely what is being suggested by the material and techniques dealt with in this book.

In the first place it should be very clearly understood what the Goddess being approached or related with consists of. Initially, she is, and will always be, the very best of every woman or female being who has ever lived, or will live, in this world. She should be considered firstly as that factor within one's closest family; next within one's racial grouping; beyond that, within one's wider geographical area; and beyond all those, as the ultimate extremity of the female principle extending throughout the whole of existence or the entirety of Cosmos itself, whatever that may be. Perhaps it should be seen as a genetic trait from the first to the last trace of femininity, covering complete creation throughout time and space—all the women who ever were, are now, and ever will be, world without end, AMEN.

To continue this theme somewhat further, the same principle could equally apply to a Father-God, who would signify all the finest qualities of individual male humans extended throughout the whole of existence. Every single soul, both male and female, would be taken as one single atom in what might be considered the mystical Body of God, or Cosmic Corpus. In other words, the ideal Deity would be composed of a perfect balanced blend between male and female atoms, comprising a Lifeforce that everyone could consider as their God.

If we have to think that far, we must also admit that the contrary could be true as well, and the worst of our natures treated in the same way would become by opposition what we might term the Devil, Satan, or whatever seems to work against our noblest instincts and impulses towards becoming the best types of beings possible. Whatever results in the nastiest and most unpleasant types of human being, both male and female.

This eternal struggle between the best and the worst in our natures, nicely mythologized as the battle between the Archangels Michael and Lucifer for the souls of humankind, is certainly factual rather than fictional. It continues in every one of us individually on one level of living, and in all of us collectively and indefinitely, until Deity decides the issue eventually. The lovely little legend concerning a huge emerald struck from Lucifer's crown falling to Earth, where it eventually became fashioned into the Holy Grail, is of considerable significance here. It was first known as the *Lapis Exilis*, literally the Stone of Exile, but its more probable meaning was *Lapis ex Coelis*, or Stone from Heaven. Suppose we make another translative split, in French this time, and make it *La pis*. What does that signify? The worst. Put all together and what do we get? The worst from Heaven. So what would that be? No less than our old enemy Lucifer, or our own evils personified. Therefore, what the Sangreal really signified was our salvation through the energies of evil being converted into the causes of good. Goethe the poet put it perfectly when he made his evil genius Mephistopheles say when questioned on his identity by Faust, "I am . . . part of the Power—misunderstood—which always evil wills, yet ever worketh good."

As a corollary to this, it might be noted that the emerald stone could be an allusion to the famous

Emerald Tablet on which all the secrets of Hermeticism were supposed to have been inscribed. Its legend says untruly that it was found in the Great Pyramid by Alexander the Great, and its well-known text describes the wonders of Heaven being reflected by those of Earth, and the Sun being the father of one particular wonder, the Moon being its mother, and the wind bearing this marvel in its womb. From thence on, whatever it was ascended to Heaven and again descended to Earth. If in Greek we take the Earth-Goddess as *Ge*, and the Sky God as *Zeus*, we have by phonetic combination the name *Je-sus* (Ge-Zeus). Moreover, if we see the concept of wind to be the "Breath of Heaven" and trace the root of "breath" to the Latin *spiritus*, we might somehow extend this to cover the idea as the Holy Spirit and so place a Christian interpretation on the whole. Green, which was taken to be the proper color of the Grail, has also become the proper liturgical color of the post-Pentecostal period, which commences from Whitsunday, or from the time when the Holy Spirit was presumed to have manifested among the faithful to commemorate the ascension of Jesus into the Heavens he was supposed to have originated from.

A parallel might be seen here between the Emerald Tablet with its "as above, so below" theme, and the Lord's Prayer, which, though paternalistic, still deals with the "as in Heaven so on Earth" hope and asks for the changing of the heavenly kingdom from celestial to mundane spheres of rulership. The prayer continues by requesting our earthly reward (bread) and forgiveness for our sins, and asks for an avoidance of evil ways by deliverance from temptation. Lastly it attributes a triple quality of omnipresence (the King-dom), omnipotence (the Power), and finally om-niscience (the Glory) to the Godhead invoked. The Emerald Tablet puts this as being the cause of all per-fection throughout the whole world, and eulogizes it as being "stronger than strength, overcoming every-thing solid, and interpenetrating everything subtle"— a kind of panacea for the ills of all humanity that sets a correct course for us to follow through every doubt and difficulty. Such was also the light in which the Sangreal was seen by those who could comprehend the mysterious metaphors and translate the terms by which it was euphemized into plainer language.

To better understand the origins of this, we shall have to go back to the times of original contact be-tween our primal selves and the space-beings that commenced our initial insemination with Blood Royal. To such orders of people, the ancient humans must have seemed more like animals, while they probably appeared like gods to our early ancestors. Though they might have only one head and four limbs like us, everything else about them would have seemed fan-tastic and unreal. They would not have smelled right, for a start, and the absence of hair on their faces and bodies would have been both puzzling and possibly frightening. Their clothing would certainly have been quite incomprehensible or even repulsive. They must have worn fabrics that were unknown on Earth at that time, or some kind of protective material that prevented the infections of Earth from reaching their skins. They may have worn face masks or breathing equipment that could adapt our atmosphere to their own requirements. Though we cannot possibly know for certain what such strange visitants may have looked like to our prototypes on this planet, we can at least be positive they would have definitely seemed altogether foreign and totally bothersome. On initial contact the humanoids would have been quite justified in considering such strangers as possibly another kind of animal, but the general concern must have been the question of possible danger. Were these newcomers hostile, and if so, to what extent? Were they life threatening in any way? That was the most important point to settle before closer contacts might be sought.

Modern imagination might well visualize the first meeting between the most primitive and the most advanced specimens of our kind on this Earth: A few of the advanced types well armored with handy concealed weapons, yet in totally nonthreatening attitudes, are sitting on the ground with outstretched hands to indicate harmlessness, while humanoid males creep gradually closer, clutching their pointed spear sticks and gripping sharp stones in poised paws. Far to the rear are chattering females, fearfully restraining their even more curious children, who are quite ready to dash forward and investigate this novel life-form that has come amongst them.

The males, meanwhile, are approaching very cautiously and slowly, making questioning noises as if to inquire intentions. The strange beings respond with unfamiliar sounds of a quiet nature, which do not seem in the least threatening. No growls, hisses, rasps, or roars. Only gentle and pleasing sounds such as a mother might soothe a fretful child with. Meanwhile the paws of these peculiar people are making the slowest and most peaceful of movements, waving very gently as if to show an absence of weaponry and openness of attitude. Several of the males drop their stones, while the boldest of them goes closer still and prods one of the strangers with his outstretched stick. The rest begin to clap their front paws and make what sounds like a noise of approval, a sort of throaty chuckle in a series of barks and cachinnations obviously intended to be friendly. The bold investigator actually puts an inquiring paw on the closest foreign body to him, but it feels so unnatural that he promptly snatches it away again in sheer surprise. The stranger then puts out its own paw and strokes the bold male's leg once or twice, upon which he extends his again and feels it being taken by the stranger's gentle grasp, accompanied by a slight squeeze and afterwards released quite quickly. One of the group then produces a very strange sort of container that is filled full of the humanoid's favorite fruit, and this is pushed towards them with a gesture that plainly means: "This is for you. We want to be friendly."

At last some of the strangers get to their feet very slowly, and one of them takes some fruit and throws it carefully in the direction of the children, and the lucky ones who grab it are soon guzzling away happily. By that time the remainder of the children reach the conclusion that the strangers are not only completely harmless but are flinging food around for free. Regardless of everything else, they rush over to their newfound friends demandingly, and are welcomed with more fruit pressed into their outstretched paws, accompanied with strokings and pattings on various parts of their anatomies, which they return by handling the very odd sort of outer skins these odd beings possess. These do not feel like proper pelts at all, but as though there is another skin beneath them. Meanwhile, seeing for themselves that their children are coming to no harm and are enjoying themselves, the women advance and begin feeling and probing for themselves, wondering why these weird creatures seem to have no genitals or excretory openings. Also why they seem so much larger and taller than Earthlings. At all events, the first contacts between humanoids and their eventual relatives on Earth were successfully established.

How long would it have taken those space visitors to complete their primary survey of our Earth ecology is very uncertain. First they needed to know if conditions here would be suitable for their type of living. That could be discovered fairly rapidly. Then they had to find out if they could interbreed their species with ours, which would certainly take several years. Because our civilization was so far behind theirs, ordinary sexual intercourse would scarcely have presented a very pleasing prospect, so it seems as if artificial insemination would have been the most likely solution. Obviously a few of their males could have fertilized quite a number of our females, but if only a few of their females were available, there would have been a correspondingly smaller proportion of Earth-male + Space-female children produced. Of those again there might have been a lesser percentage of males than females. Also assuming that the senior parents would want to remain long enough to give their offspring some kind of an initial education, at least 20 or more years would elapse in fulfilling that project. Then again it might have been that having landed here they had no means of getting away once more, so they would have to stay here until they all died and their children reached the third generation. By that time the Sangreal strain of bloodstock would have commenced its continuity mostly through the females fertilized by the more prolific original male suppliers of seed. By that time the surviving offspring should have been able to breed in the natural way, since they had grown up with each other and become accustomed to their conditions.

Nevertheless, for quite a long time there would have been a normal tendency for such humanoid-plus people to mate solely amongst themselves, which would of course have established the Sangreal strain as a gene in its own right, after which it was purely a question of time before it commenced to spread throughout the remainder of the race until it became as it is today—worldwide yet still varying considerably in degree and concentration. However, there remains that particular factor in ourselves that accounts for our development and steadily advancing levels of intelligence, leading us towards our ultimate human destiny. We might as well call this the God-Goddess factor in ourselves, because that is what it amounts to. Whatever else it might be, this Sangreal strain is the Divine Drive or inmost urge impelling us along a path of progression we can scarcely avoid following in search of our future fate.

At this present point along that strange path, those scriptural and often quoted words are coming true, and having eaten of the Tree of Knowledge, which taught us to distinguish between good and evil, we are indeed becoming as the gods for some other unfortunate world where we will eventually seed our species, letting them care for their own conduct and civilization with only the genetically carried memories of ourselves to guide them as their gods. For their sake as much as our own, let us hope they will make a much better job of civilizing themselves in their world than we have done with ours.

Since our preoccupation with a male-dominated Godhead has resulted in so many disastrous and totally wasteful wars amongst us, we had better pray wholeheartedly that any future God-ideas will result only in concepts of a Being with correctly balanced proportions of each polarity. It is probably unwise to speculate at present concerning the exact proportions required to blend a perfect sort of spiritual Power or ideal Image, but let us assume for hypothetical purposes a 50–50 mixture of male-female potentials. Granted, our current ideas of theoretical Deity are virtually those of a sexless Energy operating by means of a superconsciousness we cannot at present comprehend, but what makes us suppose that such would be a satisfactory concept to impose on anyone's ideology? Basically we have to admit that any ideas we may hold concerning the nature of Deity must be purely transitional, or those which we find most suitable at any given period of our evolution. Hitherto we have regarded our concepts of Deity to be conclusive, but it is surely time we altered any immutable ideas to include others of a more adaptable kind.

Most people are familiar with the law of nature that has been framed as "adapt—or die." This might otherwise be put, "change—or cease," and it applies in all areas human or divine. The art of magic was once defined as "causing change in conformity with Will." Living creatures that could adapt with changing conditions survived, and those that either would or could not, perished. Adaptation or necessary alteration is the main message conveyed by the Emerald Tablet, and it means that we should discover the secrets of changing ourselves and our natures to conform with whatever consciousness may be affecting us through its force-fields. Since the principal power affecting our lives on Earth derives from the concepts we make of Deity, that is what we shall need to adapt with in some mutually satisfying style so as to continue our living with some degree of reasonable comfort.

All changes take place at a certain *rate* or quantity and intensity in relation to time needed to effect such a change properly. That is just as true in the case of ideas and awareness as it might be about anything else. There is an ideal rate for any change required, whatever it might be. Excess or insufficiency could be damaging or possibly fatal to any type of operation involving serious changes. Just as there is an ideal speed limit governing a motor's rate of physical progress along our roads, so there is a comparably ideal rate for safe progress of the thoughts and feelings passing through the sense-tracks of our souls. Though we cannot possibly measure these with anything like the accuracy of material things, it could be reasonable to assume that the deeper and more serious the nature of anything is, then the more slowly it should be made in order to ensure its subsequent satisfactory condition.

So to change our ideas concerning the nature of our Godhead needs time, but if it is also something that needs doing, we will want some assurance that such a process is being instituted and will proceed at a safe and proper rate of progress according to our current capabilities. The progression could be a lot faster than in former times, since we have speeded everything up so much during our present period. Nevertheless it still takes nine months to develop a baby properly, from a tiny blob of pulsating jelly to a miniature human being, and yet during those nine months several millions of years of evolution have to be recapitulated and compressed into what might seem like a split second by comparison. To continue this theme, we have to take that baby and later subject it to a stream of consciousness which has taken its fellow mortals several thousand years to construct into a comprehensive whole that is suitable for bringing out reasonable responses from the natural intelligence latent in each child's genes, and these will vary from one individual to another according to the IQ concerned. That factor is what we have been considering as being connected with the Sangreal strain, or our original impetus in the direction of Deity regarded as the result of evolutionary experience.

One immediate concern that is sure to arise at some point is whether the encouragement of forming a feminine Goddess-Ideal will not promote homosexuality among males. The rational response to this concern is that homosexuality per se is nothing more than a natural inclination amongst intelligent males to seek sexual satisfaction amongst each other in a grossly overpopulated society. In other words, they sense that the human herd in which they live has become far too numerous for civilized comfort or economic security, and their instincts allow them only two options: murder enough other males to permit themselves sufficient living space, or come to friendly terms with them on socio-sexual levels. One might call this the "kiss or kill" option due to people-pressure, and which is the more preferable of the two is open to anyone's opinion.

Another alternative is to maintain infertile sex partnerships with those willing to participate in them, or to seek sexual satisfaction with substitutes for human beings, but such would only appeal to a minority of people. The majority need is for close human companionship with a compatible mate preferably having sympathetic interests. Original objections to homosexuality arose entirely from deep-seated fears that it threatened the human fertility factor and so endangered our species and everyone else's opportunities for evolution. There was also an instinctive feeling that traces of the masculine Sangreal strain might be lost forever, which would indeed have been a serious setback for humanity. Once it became obvious that little short of mass extinction was likely to menace the multiplication of humankind, attitudes began to change, and certainly with Greek civilization, homosexuality was regarded in a more reasonable light.

With all herd animals, including humans, it is a normal process for young males in season to fight and possibly kill each other for the privilege of access to fertile females. This is actually only a repetition of the sperm-behavior pattern that results in a contest for survival amongst all the sperms injected, so that in the end only one is successful in winning its way to the egg. Perhaps we might be reminded of the melee or free-for-all fight in the medieval tournaments, where lustful young knights would compete for the coveted guerdon from the hands of the fairest maid selected by popular choice. However, those were the times when the Holy Grail legends flourished, and no legend without some truth in it ever survives as long as that one has done in the West.

That the Grail per se was a mainly feminine objective there need be no doubt at all. There are far too many literary nudges and hints in that direction, plus all the surrounding symbology employed. It was at that period, too, when the peculiar concept of "courtly love" arose in connection with idealized sex, which was previously undreamed of amongst normal noble Westerners. It was the nearest they might come to the worship of Woman as an ideal for its own sake, thus raising the roughest class of men to the worthiest type of gentleman without actually arousing the antagonism of the Holy Church, which was usually ready to rear up at any hard hints of heresy. It was considered quite normal amongst Eastern cultures for a female to seek her God in her husband while he sought his Goddess in her, but propagating those kind of ideas with Westerners subject to rigid religious rules was quite a different prospect altogether.

So the Grail-suggested cult of courtly love became

regarded as a kind of social game played for pleasure only on its surface, yet which could be interpreted on much deeper levels by those who knew and followed its rules. Those were set out in such a way as to offer no offense to religious dogmatists, yet they afforded every opportunity to those choosing an alternative ideology. For example, the Tarot pack of cards was produced as what seemed like a harmless gambling game, yet it consisted of four suits (from the French *ensuite* = following) showing the Grail "hallows" of the Cup and Platter to indicate femininity, and the penile Spear and Sword for masculinity; then came a "people pack" of two senior and two junior males with the same number of matching females. This alone illustrated the idea of equality between the sexes. Supporting such a set came 22 Triumph (or Trump) cards, each of which was a concept relative to the basic beliefs in life at that period. The fact that this collection could be aligned with the Qabbalistic Tree of Life, plus the probability of the word "Tarot" being derived from two Hebrew words signifying "to mark out present or possible happenings" seems to point towards Middle Eastern mystics as its originators.

However, the Tarot was only part of the picture. The general idea of courtly love was that a male would select, with her full permission and encouragement, some noble lady who would act as his ideal of womanhood. She would then try to become an epitome of all the virtues and graces he proposed to worship as best he could. He might compose songs and verses in her honor, impose all sorts of tasks and obligations on himself or undertake those proposed by her, doing everything he could think of to please her and attract her favorable attention. He was supposed to languish for her love, while she kept him in a constant state of anticipation of enjoyments she should never permit factually. That is to say, she was supposed to maintain him in a permanent condition of sexual excitement without ever gratifying him completely. To us this might sound like pointless sado-masochism, but to the medieval mind it seemed like a pleasing proposition based on socio-religious practice. Modern minds might suppose the whole maneuver was more like a small boy trying to gain his mother's approval.

The operative proposition covering this entire custom was that Woman would and should be the natural salvation of Man, since she had contributed so greatly to his "fall." It has since been the obligation of women to civilize, educate, and culture humankind. His reward in return for all her good influences was the privilege of serving her with a very special sort of love far above the usual carnal kind, being demonstrable of sexual service on a very high spiritual scale, hence there should be no physical sexual intercourse to debase such a noble relationship. Among the German exponents of this novel art, it was known as "Minne" or High Love, and a custom arose among them called "Minnetrinken," or drinking to the ideal of Minne with wine in which a few drops of their blood had been mingled. This was taken with sacramental solemnity.

Although in the main this movement was more or less confined to the aristocracy of certain European countries, notably France and Germany, and to a lesser extent elsewhere, its ideology did play an important part in the elevation of women to a far higher status than formerly. There was also the custom known as the *droit du seigneur*, or the then-recognized right of the local lord to enjoy any female peasant on his estate for the first time on the occasion of her legal marriage. This custom had nothing to do with sex delights for wicked lordlings with innocent virgins. It was a solemn obligation enjoined on the nobility to "pass on the Blood" amongst those less fortunate than themselves. Moreover it was considered a very great honor to foster children begotten by an undoubted nobleman, and these would become privileged people when they grew up. In fact this was the origin of that famous phrase *noblesse oblige*, or "nobility has its obligations." The principles of good breeding were very well known, and indeed were carried to the early plantations in the New World, where slave owners would beget half-caste children on their favored female servants. The end effects of this are still evident throughout the Americas today.

Breeding good livestock is something that has been well understood and practiced for a very long time. In very ancient times marriage between important families would sometimes be decided by a very primitive blood test that consisted in blood being drawn from the wrists of the prospective bride and groom and mingled, then the results would be carefully observed by those claiming an ability to pronounce a final judgment. If when the two pools of blood met, they flowed together immediately and appeared to accept each other without any hesitation, no ban would be pronounced on the marriage. Conversely, should there seem to be any reluctance to mingle freely, or one blood was seen as distinct from the other after attempts had been made to combine them, such a sign would be taken as a positive act of prohibition against mating the couple concerned. There is a relic of this primitive practice today in the legal necessity of a blood test by those proposing marriage to each other in most American states so as to produce evidence of freedom from hereditary or congenital syphiletic disorders. Hopefully this will be eventually extended to include AIDS as well. There is also a symbolic trace of the custom left in some Christian churches in the momentary binding of the couple's wrists together by the stole of the priest who marries them.

Earlier generations of physicians attached great importance to the factor of heredity, inquiring into the prevalence of specific diseases "in the family" and whether this might be on the male or the female side. Then followed a period during which it was fashionable to pooh-pooh such outmoded outlooks and ascribe everything to "environmentalism." However, since the days of genetic engineering, we have gone back to the older and wiser belief of regarding both bodily and mental behaviors as being typical of the genetic traits that began and developed them. In times to come there are bound to be discoveries that will lead to certain knowledge concerning ideal gene-combinations, resulting in the most perfect types of humans.

Nevertheless, human beings do not begin with the physical part of the sexual act but with the thinking and feeling that precedes that act and so to speak materializes it. None of us are purely the product of our parents' bodies but of their minds and souls as well. Some schools of thought would say that the greater part of ourselves came from such a source than merely from its mortal counterpart. Our bodies may be a physical convenience allowing our individuated consciousness to function in this world, but which would most thinking people regard as being ME—their bodies or their sentient selves that activate that body, motivate it meaningfully, and order its behavior in accordance with intention? If the major part of anyone's ME is derived from their parents' spiritual selves (which derives from their parents ad infinitum), and the greater part of that again comes from a feminine type of consciousness, we had best think what might be done with this in our own times.

Chapter Four

Matriarchal Meanings

Conceiving an ideal Goddess depends on whether it is done from a male or female viewpoint. Since males must naturally include the sexual element, which none but female homosexuals would accept, the only mutual relationships worth considering are those of mother, sister, daughter, or friend. The category of friend is a relatively recent one, since pure friendship between a man and a woman was a rare factor prior to a few short centuries ago, and even now might not be considered possible in some strict countries. For an orthodox Muslim to introduce a wife to a masculine acquaintance would be regarded as insulting or offensive, yet both men might enjoy the company of professional women entertainers paid for supplying sexual stimuli. In fact, the publicans whom Jesus was reproached for keeping company with in his time were known as *publica puella*, or public girls, because their services were available to anyone hiring them. Prostitution has long been known as the oldest profession in the world, and many centuries were to elapse before women might claim professional relationships with men on the grounds of educational, cultural, or technical abilities alone.

Gautama Buddha, on being questioned by a monk as to how one should deal with women, replied that age alone decided the matter. If older than the querent, she would be regarded as a mother, if of the same age group, then as a sister, but if younger, as a daughter. In other words, as a female relative with whom sexual contact would not normally be permissible. Although brother and sister marriages were believed to be allowable by some cultures, interbreeding among close relatives was strongly discouraged by many others, who had come to the conclusion that such was a bad practice unlikely to improve the genetic stock and much more probably to spoil it very badly. The Christian Church in particular imposed very strict rulings about marriage within what were called forbidden degrees of kindred, some quite beyond limits that modern geneticists might consider reasonable. Besides, the Church approved of "passing on the Blood" as far afield as possible, although by that time marriage between recognized noble houses and those who might only claim mercantile status was by no means exceptional.

To idealize the Eternal Feminine as a mother or sister or daughter alone is scarcely feasible unless one postulates a father also, which immediately opens up the possibility of extended relationships throughout the whole of existence. If, however, one takes up the standard of a celibate personage, thus eliminating the wifely or daughterly element, then a purely maternal relationship with an idealized Deity can quite well be conceived, which was why several orders of priesthood advocated celibacy as a rule to be observed by its masculine members. Maybe the most noticeable of these was the priesthood of Cybele, who devoted themselves to their concept of Deity by voluntary castration, which was the supreme sacrifice short of life itself that any mortal male may make.

The concept of this Goddess is most significant. She was said to be the daughter of Heaven (Zeus) and Earth (Ge) who became the mate of Chronos-Saturn (Time), and she was equated with most Mother-Goddess aspects. She became enamored with Atys, a beautiful Phrygian youth whom she persuaded to devote to perpetual chastity and celibacy. He soon broke this vow with a lovely nymph, Sangaris (best blood?), which so infuriated Cybele that she provoked Atys into castrating himself with a sharp flint, whereupon Cybele changed him into a pine tree, which was ever afterwards sacred to the Mother of the Gods. Her priests were supposed to convert themselves into eunuchs by an awesome rite of self-mutilation involving removal of their testicles with an ancient flint knife such as were still traditional for the killing of a Sacred King.

First the neck of the scrotum was tightly ligatured, after which all present in the temple danced themselves into a state of delirium, aided by drugs and drumming accompanied by much banging of spears on shields and howling of human comrades. It must have sounded something like a modern disco session. This hideous racket was supposed to symbolize the

Goddess mourning for her lost lover, but it might equally have meant him bewailing his missing manhood. At the climax of this cacophony, a specially shaped wooden block was placed on the stone altar and the neck of the scrotum severed with as few strokes as possible. He would then be attended by brother priests, who had to staunch any bleeding, probably make more noise to drown his howls, then bring the service to a satisfactory conclusion as best they could.

Worship of Cybele must have been very popular or there would not have been so many temples dedicated to her. We are told that her particular type of worship was of a purely orgiastic nature, but it probably served a strong psychological need amongst her devotees. The old word *orgy* means "secret rites," and there is also a connection with *oregon*, a priest, and *orego*, meaning an impulse or feeling, especially rage and anger. Then again, *orgao*, as applied to animals, meant to swell, to be in heat, or to be excited and passionate. Every one of these implications signified sexual arousal.

Probably the principal function of a Cybelean temple of olden days was to work off sexual and similar frustrations that might have otherwise warped human souls very badly. Surely everyone must have thought at some time in their lives how wonderful it would be to have some place where they would be allowed to "let it all hang out" and throw away all inhibitions while behaving in any way acceptable to those present—complete freedom to prance around stark naked or clothed in any weird way pleasing the wearer. There would obviously have to be some kind of a behavior code that would prevent sheer savagery or wanton destruction, but up to that limit people could please themselves entirely. There would be complete freedom to proclaim any personal secret at the top of one's voice without fear of criticism, condemnation, or anyone trying to capitalize on it by blackmail. Such might sound like an eighteenth-century madhouse or a twentieth-century football field, but there need be no doubt of its emotionally liberating nature.

By sacrificing their gonads, the Cybelean priests believed they were converting themselves into the closest human substitutes for females—namely, infertile males. How far they realized that their natures were altering because of hormonal deprivation is dubious, but that they knew a change would take place in their characters subsequent to their sacrifice seems certain enough. The evidence of change in their vocal tones alone was indisputable, since it feminized their voices remarkably, which probably gave rise to the sexual suppositions. Though it later became obligatory for applicants to the Christian priesthood to prove their non-Cybelean status by showing their testicles to a bishop prior to their ordination, a special order of chorister known as the castrati was once welcome in the Sistine Chapel at Rome. The amazing alto quality of their superb singing became world famous.

Although the physical facts concerning sex change and its normal consequences are now not only very well known but also surgically possible, what we should be looking for is an alteration of *ideals* from a male to a female focus and past that again to a God concept of unique design—a balanced and harmonious combination of both polarities, each distinct in its own right, yet capable of exerting energy-effects when applied together as a single spiritual source of perfect Power. All those preconditions would be entirely true if the Deity we desired were electricity, which is a single force consisting of a dual potency applied simultaneously to produce a calculated result.

Are we suggesting here that electricity is an ideal example of the way in which we should construct our Goddess concept? Why not? Such would be one of our most ancient images brought up to date. In olden times people saw a thunderstorm as a complete sex act between the Sky God and the Earth Goddess. First there would be a feeling of tension in the air while everything seemed hot and heavy and the sky got darker and darker as their God lay more heavily over their land. Following a few little drops of leakage, there would be a sudden roar of released feelings, and his fearful phallus of fire would stab with incredible speed deep into the embracing Earth. Floods and floods of his regenerating sperm would pour into her welcoming womb, and time after time that fearful phallus would plunge itself into the groaning Goddess. Heaven help any luckless human who got in the way of that all-powerful weapon, because they would be burned to a cinder. Was that not how fire first came to them—in a fearful flash that set the trees alight, after which bold men picked up burning branches and set fire to other things with the flames? Eventually after the Sky God was satisfied, he would roll off the drenched Goddess and retreat to the Sun once more, leaving her steaming gently in warm, wet comfort. Later on the seeds implanted in her would grow up to provide fruit and grain for the people to eat. Great indeed were the Gods and Goddesses who could work such wonders.

Today we are apt to smile at what seems to us such childish simplicity, but that particular concept is surely far too beautiful to inspire anything but sympathetic feelings of fellowship from sincerely sensitive people. A twentieth-century B.C. man sees God-sex in a thunderstorm, and a twentieth-century A.D. man cuts a sex symbol from his girlie magazine and sticks it on the wall near his bed to stimulate his masturbation fantasies. What is the difference? Only time and custom. To both men, 40 centuries apart, sex represents a control force in their respective lives. One identifies it as a God-Goddess concept even if those words would mean nothing to him, while the other sees it as an immediate personal need to be satisfied through sensation. Maybe the modern man's viewpoint has become more limited than that of his far-distant confrere, since he knows quite well that his sex-satisfaction will only be a temporary affair calling for repetitions at intervals; whereas his earlier ancestor saw Deity as someone far greater than himself who would always be available on proper application. Deciding which man made the most from his own ideology is a moot point to be considered very carefully.

By divorcing our current concepts of Deity from any trace of sexual significance, we have done ourselves a serious disservice, since we have deprived our social cultures of a major motive in life on a spiritual scale. This of course refers mostly to Western religions and philosophies. Orientals have retained their sexual

God-Goddess concepts, which could account for the popularity of Eastern mysticism among young and sexually active Westerners feeling a need for worship of an active ideal. Let them be assured that the old Deities of the Western world have by no means departed from us but have only hidden themselves behind screens of misrepresentation put up by those who would rather see everything in ways other than those of our earlier imaginings. What we are actually looking at are only pictures put up by other mortal minds than ours, and if we want to see the same fundamental truths in any sort of a different light, then it remains for us to switch that illumination on and just continue looking. The oldest of our male-female Deity concepts will always remain where they were in the first place: inside ourselves awaiting our most recent attention.

Whoever thinks about the nature of electricity when they switch their house lights on? Yet who could calculate the total amount of human thinking that had to be expended by how many minds before electric lights became possible only in the last century? Who thinks about the principles of aerodynamics and the mechanisms using them when sitting in an aircraft during some intercontinental flight? Again, we are profiting from the amazing amounts of intelligent thinking that had to be done for sometimes centuries of time before it all emerged as a practical product we could enrich our existence with. This is just as true for a Deity concept as for any other production of our imaginative faculties, unless we were content to invoke Deity as an unknown Energy taken for granted because of other people's belief in It.

In fact, such is the basis for the religious beliefs or practices of many millions of human beings. As children they were told that their deities were thus and so, and that they should behave in such a way or say prayers in this or that fashion. They are taught some specific behavior pattern to be observed either in private or public, and then frequently left to make what they want out of that. To most children this is partly a new game, but more importantly it is an evocation of genetic memories implanted deep within themselves, brought to the surface by their parents' and relatives' promptings. Later in life they will find that much of this will have altered due to their subconscious activities and rationalizations, but there will always be a residue left from their earliest genetic indoctrinations, which could be worked with if they were really interested in doing so and progressing past the point of whatever potential had already been implanted. Relatively few people are sufficiently keen to improve upon their childhood impressions of Deity, and are satisfied to accept those purely as a basis for subsequent substitutions by their own inquiring minds. Therefore they have done very little to alter or improve our collective store of spiritual consciousness.

There are, however, always a certain proportion of souls who have an inquisitive nature concerning their less material selves and the esoteric energies affecting them. Such a static leave-well-alone attitude will never satisfy them in the least, and so they continue probing and searching into the normally concealed side of living experience until they find something to think about and examine, which might afford some kind of an answer to at least some part of their problems. These are the types of souls, it is hoped, who may be intrigued enough by the material offered in this and similar works to enter their own "Secret Places" and dig out the Deity ideas hiding in their concealed identities. Not only that, but once such are even suspected, to make meaningful relationships with these and encourage them to explain themselves in comprehensible terms. Even if only a slight degree of such self-discovery is obtainable, that would still make a useful contribution to the sum total of human spiritual experience.

If anyone should seriously consider constructing a workable Deity concept of either a masculine, a feminine or a combined character, they had better go back to the idea of making magical circles of consciousness around themselves, with each covering a category of their fellow beings in relation to themselves. The idea is to begin with oneself as if one were the nucleus of an atom with realms of rulership around oneself extending indefinitely—something like the sun of a solar system with each planetary orbit meaning another particular collection of people. This means to say, to set up and operate a cosmic pattern of Consciousness. It could be noticed here that the basic idea of circling represents a great many important images—a living cell, the zodiac or seasonal cycle, the Wheel of birth and death, a power circuit, endless eternity, a containment of Consciousness, the Cosmic Cross—whatever the idea of a circle suggests to anyone working within it.

The operative idea is similar to that once used by schoolboys to write their addresses, just to show what big ideas they had of themselves. For example: John

Doe, 3205 Lilac Street, Queens, New York, New York State, North America, the world, the solar system, the universe, SPACE. In this case the immediate circle outside oneself is the closest family of blood relations. All who can be thought of as living or dead should be called to mind and visualized as comprising the inmost circle. Those known personally can be clearly imagined, and those not quite so well known, remembered from photographs. The important thing is to place those most directly related by blood the nearest: mother, father, brothers, and sisters, husbands and wives, uncles and aunts, and cousins, then grandparents with their relatives behind those again. They all should constitute quite a little crowd. At first they will have to be built up one by one from the memory banks of the brain, but later, after they have become a clear and composite picture, a single conscious command should summon awareness of them all as a complete unity. Perhaps the operative word FAMILY would be sufficient. It is very important that the same command words be used on each occasion this exercise is performed. As the relationship gets more distant, people may be imagined increasingly vaguely until they become just a blur, although a bigger and bigger one accordingly.

The next circle should consist of friends, again living or dead, near or remote in residence. Their order of connection should be according to their degree of relationship with whoever is working this exercise from the center. By this time it should be seen that these imaginary circles are more theoretical than practical, since some close friends will mean a lot more to the operator than possibly very close blood relatives. Similarly, dead friends might seem more important than living ones, so they should take precedence of place. The governing factor in the whole of this process must always be that of significance to the operator. After the initial construction of this circle, the command word FRIENDS should be sufficient to summon it entirely with one single sweep of imaginative interest.

Since the ensuing circles of fellow humans will be those unknown from personal experience, they will have to be "blocked in" fairly quickly, yet they must at all costs be taken into account because they form a part of the personal perimeter that has or has had an active effect on the life of whoever is invoking them. The closest will obviously be fellow blood beings who have caused any sorts of change within the entire grouping: inventors, writers, thinkers, or doers who have added even the slightest iota to the self-state of all concerned; plus of course those who have kept such factors going and have altered or advanced them in any way. By this time we should be running into millions of mortals, who can be classed under the general heading of FELLOW FOLK.

Although it should be easily recognized that in the course of nature there would be a series of circles extending indefinitely outward that included the whole of humanity past, present, and future, the first three categories should be quite sufficient to handle with a general acknowledgment made in the direction of all outsiders under the collective yet inclusive category FOREIGNERS.

Under those four main thought categories everyone other than the thinker can be called up into conscious relationship in a matter of moments and considered as an entirety centered on a single being. It should be specially noted that none are classed as enemies or as having hostile intentions, although such would undoubtedly exist in real life. Nevertheless those should always be considered as a minority element outweighed in importance by an overwhelming majority of nonantagonistic people. The main point to bear in mind is that the whole of such an incredible mass of human beings are, or have been, sentient souls whose consciousness in relationship to oneself has influenced one's existence in some way, and has therefore helped to create an identity separate from, yet permanently connected with, their own. To that extent, *we are each other*.

No reasonable person would deny that the energies generated by the thoughts and feelings of all those forenamed human beings constitute a real and actual Force that we might identify with our Deity, since it directs our lives in common. Because all forces are polarized power, we can surely postulate both positive and negative qualities as being essential to its nature. While it would be quite inaccurate to equate positive with male and negative with female polarities, since either sex uses both ends of the same Energy according to needs, we do require some degree of definition in order to rationalize our thinking. We might therefore consider positive as something surplus or emissive in character that passes *from* anything *to* something else and is symbolized by +. Yet why should that be so? Simply because its surplus is supplied from the negative potential, which thus becomes a deficiency requiring an intake to fulfill its need for supplies of energy, and so it is symbolized by –. So plus (+) and minus (–) are really states or conditions existing in anything at any given instant, but the important thing to remember is that one cannot exist without the other any more than a left could exist without a right. Power always implies a pair of principles to make it so, and each should be equally effective.

A purely feminine Deity concept would be just as futile as our present masculinized one, but because there is so strong a need for her, that means a negative condition is inviting a positive impulse to equalize it. Perhaps this indicates that we ought to strengthen our attention to Deity from a feminine angle while awakening it from a masculine one, but the clear intimation is that a commonly acceptable Deity concept should be found by males and females of our world that combines the best qualities of both and the ideal aims of either. Possibly the reason why our ideal Goddess has been seen mainly as a Mother figure is because it would be about the only aspect equally approachable by males and females alike if confined to that relationship alone, unless the possibility of a Friend category, which would be held in common, is also admitted.

How should we start conceiving this ideal Mother image? Preferably this should be done by intelligent adults who are familiar with the culture of their own traditions, who love nature, who have at least an acquaintance with the arts, and who are of good health and have opportunities for periods of contemplation.

It is not really necessary to wear any sort of robes unless particularly inclined to select something for that purpose, but there certainly ought to be some definite symbol to indicate intention of mind during the time spent concentrating on the concept. Perhaps this might be a ring or a pectoral hung around the neck, a bracelet on the wrist, or some special pin attached to the clothing—even a colored cord around the waist—whatever it may be, the thing should be formally dedicated to its purpose with words something in this style:

"Blessed be this_____. May it be for me a means of meeting my Bloodbeing as a mother, mind to mind and soul to soul. Let this lead me to her through whichever ways I shall be taught to take by the most blessed blood of our beliefs. So guide me, Goddess, in my special search for spiritual goodness, amen."

Similar formulae may be used for anything else required in this quest. The particular principle to observe scrupulously is that whatever may be made or dedicated to this Deity-discovery purpose should never be used for anything else whatsoever. This applies especially to the next artifact, which is a composite picture of the Mystical Mother, with a smaller picture of the seeker's own mother in the center of the foreground, and flanked if possible by still smaller pictures of both grandmothers. Since no one can know for certain what the Mother concept should look like, everyone must select their own idea, which should preferably be an artist's representation rather than the likeness of a living person. Unless anyone has the talent to paint such a picture themselves, this could involve photocopying from a collection of likely artistic impressions.

The finished production should be of a convenient size to handle, say about 8 x 5 inches, and a fitting frame should be found for it. The best proportions should probably be so that the face, neck, and shoulders of the selected ideal Being fill up the frame, while the smaller parental pictures occupy the neck space of the image itself. The correct symbolism for the frame would be an oval one indicative of feminine or vaginal character. On no account should a square or oblong frame be employed to display a Mother concept.

Once this symbol has been found and brought to a satisfactory state of suggestive significance, the next thing to settle on is its aural equivalent. What sound suggests mothers most? People are apt to vary considerably on this point, but if there is any special tune with a definite Mother-meaning in it for anyone, then that would be a suitable one for that particular person to select. However, there is no need to choose any special tune when there are so many other sounds indicative of motherhood. What about seashore sounds or the ripple of wavelets against the sides of a boat? Humming or heartbeats? Maybe the breathing noises heard while we were still in our mothers' wombs? Quite a good tape can be made from natural sounds collected during an ordinary excursion into the country.

Scent should also be used suggestively. Though the immediate impulse might be to employ ordinary domestic odors, it is better to use something of a more spiritual significance, such as floral scents. Probably the best thing to settle for is a potpourri of pomander that can be easily applied to the nose whenever required. The important thing here is that whatever scent may be chosen should thenceforth only be used for Mother concept exercises alone.

When it comes to finding a taste-symbol to suit maternal meditations, milk seems the most likely one, although the least attractive. However, since we are metaphorically related Bloodbeings in maternal guise, any red-colored and pleasantly flavored fruit juice or table wine should serve as a symbol, and it ought to be sucked through a straw to remind the drinker of how food-fluid was once imbibed from a mother's breast.

Dealing with the final sense, touch, a Masonic type of apron seems the most appropriate thing to wear. Aprons are certainly mother-associated for all sorts of reasons. They are used not only as protective garments during domestic duties but also as padding to wrap around infants' loins to prevent them from soiling anything. We might also remember that in the Masonic movement, whatever lodge a member first joins is always known as his Mother Lodge, because that was where he first "saw the Light" and was "born into the Brotherhood." There also is the Christian reference to the necessity of being born again before there can be any hope of entering the Kingdom of God, which implies the need of a spiritual Mother in some sense. The Church was always referring to itself as a Mother regarding its members, who were presumed to be "children." So if a common article such as an apron can suggest Motherhood to the touch, why not accept this and let it signify that important Ideal? There is no need to employ an actual Masonic type of apron, since simple substitutes can be easily made from any type of cloth or plastic material, provided it covers the knees while sitting with the hands resting on it so that it can be felt with the fingers.

Once all the five symbols are assembled together, they can soon be combined to make interesting and valuable esoteric exercises. First a program must be decided upon to structure the scheme. Regularity and intensive action are the main requirements. It is better to devote five minutes a day with sufficient strength of concentrated consciousness than to spend two hours every week in uncertainty and distraction. If it should be difficult to maintain clear concentration at first, try giving direct orders to the mind by saying something like:

"Stray thinking stop. Do not distract me from the theme that I have chosen for my present frame of mind. Let this Mother-thinking be my sole concern for these few moments. Whatsoever is of Her I welcome in. Other thoughts I order out until I choose to readmit them. Be this so forthwith."

It is amazing how the average mind will obey orders given authoritatively and unequivocably in that fashion.

If the location can be the same for every exercise, so much the better; but if not, the symbols are small enough to be carried on the person and set up almost anywhere. Ten minutes at a time is quite sufficient for the first few exercises, and they should not last much longer than that in any case. If any definite formulae are needed for commencing and concluding each session, these might well be made in this way. At the beginning:

"Be a blessing bidden on this spiritual search for my most mystic Mother and my true Bloodbeing. Amen." And then at the end: *Thanks be unto the Mother motivating me that I have taken one more step towards the truth I surely am in spirit. Amen."*

The actual working itself should consist in setting up the symbols close to oneself, with the picture where it can be clearly seen from the chair on which one sits. Nearby should be a table on which are placed the drink and the pomander together with the tape recorder, which should have enough tape in it to last as long as needed. The hands should be left loosely on the knees, where they can feel the fabric of the apron, and the illumination of the place ought to be arranged suitably. Perhaps the picture could be spotlighted while everything else stays in shadow; or as a refinement, soft impulsive effects coinciding with a human heartbeat might be made with an electromechanism. To suggest pre-birth conditions, the light could be faintly red, such as a fetus might observe if a powerful light were shown on its mother's abdomen. When all has been set in operative order, a commencement is made by calling up the four circles around oneself with their command words while realizing that a common bond of blood exists between all those millions of souls called to consciousness, the closest being very strong and those furthest away correspondingly weak; yet so long as there is even the most minimal trace existing, a linkage of Love should still be perceptible to spiritual sight. As a people, we are all products of that same wonderful Womb belonging to the Being we consider our Bloodmother. Once that idea can be appreciated properly, the picture should be concentrated on, and thinking continued something like this:

"I am looking at a picture of my last mortal mother with my idea of my first spiritual one, who is a long way behind her, and who is present in all mothers in between—many millions of them, and yet only One as an Idea—all linked together by an infinitely long line of blood. Connecting with that line are who knows how many others, who make up my spiritual family by our mystical blood relationship. We may not know each other consciously or individually, yet because of our common Mother we are all brethren. I send my thoughts to everyone who senses this and greet you very gladly. We are upon this planet to benefit one another because of what we think and do together. We are here and we are human beings for a mutual purpose, which we will indeed fulfill, so far as we are able. So let us duly do what destiny decrees, and may we meet together at the end of time when we will keep our final tryst with Truth."

Occasional sniffs at the pomander may be made during this meditation, after which an affirmative invocation should be stated clearly, either aloud or mentally:

"Bloodbeing meet my questing mind, I shall seek and we will find, when we link with one another, you your child and I my Mother."

Next follows another direct approach to the Concept, which takes this standpoint:

"Mystical Mother I am your descendant through a lengthy line of mortal mothers, and as each one died, so you

continued as a Concept who conceived us all and made your-self the Matrix out of which our species have been molded and maintained until the present period. Now I need to know you consciously myself and so become aware of what and whom you are as an assurance that my spiritual future will be made secure within your wonderful and welcome womb. Show me what I should know, which will encourage and sustain me in my search for everlasting entity and ultimate enlightenment in PERFECT PEACE PROFOUND."

After a short silent pause, say:

"I summon you in spirit by the Blood that you began and is in me begetting. Be there love between us all as our most precious link with life."

At this point the drink is blessed and partaken of. Although any appropriate formula will serve, a good standard one is,

"Be this our Motherblood that through it we may meet our true Bloodmother."

The drink need not be drunk at a single draught but may be sipped quite slowly while thinking of the significance of what has been happening: One human soul has realized its own deepest and most ancient roots, sunk in spiritual rather than material soil, and it is reaching for these with every possible sincerity. We know perfectly well that we cannot recognize our mightiest Mother as she really is, and so we have contrived these symbols to act as agencies for our consciousness to use aspiringly. We are seeing her as a personification of pure Power, with all the attributes of motherhood ascribed to her for the perpetuation of all people and ours in particular. As Western souls, we believe that our blood began with what we call the Sangreal, and that it will end with everyone else's in true enlightenment. After contemplating this, the invocant must reach inside him/herself and say or think with a maximum of meaning:

"Come Mother of my blood; communicate with me thy child."

Then concentrate as intently as possible while awaiting an inner response. This might be nothing more than a momentary impression or an instinctive feeling that something or Someone is trying to make contact. There is no point in trying to force a closer or clearer sense of spiritual stirrings within oneself. Whatever comes must do so of its own accord, however it means to. Simply maintain an open attitude of invitation and that is all. After waiting patiently a few moments, the exercise should be terminated with the following phrase or an equivalent:

"As this external effort ends, the quest continues constantly. Working and waiting accomplishes all, so as I have worked I will now wait and patiently pursue my aim of making closer contact with my own Bloodbeing."

Such is the structure of a ceremony designed to appreciate the reality of our most powerful female parent as a Deity concept. Ideally such sessions should take place several times a week for the first few months, but the fundamental format ought always to follow the same pattern, the sequence of which is (1) initial arrangement and invocation, (2) general meditation, (3) direct personal invocation, (4) direct mediation, (5) blood communion, (6) meditation thereupon, (7) receptivity period, and (8) conclusion.

It might be as well to mention here what the old-time magi used to call the License of the Spirits to Depart, usually meaning a long and solemn exhortation full of "do's and don'ts" together with a lot of instructions that the supposed spirits were to obey faithfully and without any arguments. There was actually quite a good reason for this from a psychological viewpoint, which anyone familiar with hypnotism should recognize in a moment. That is the needed *status quo ante* suggestion, which means putting the mind back into the state it was prior to all the suggestions intended to alter its awareness. Since we began by calling up our four circles of connected humanity, we should put them back where they came from with a grateful acknowledgment. Politeness is always advised towards "spirits," even if they are one's own thoughts. It is a good policy to adopt anyway, unless there is some definite reason otherwise. So the last thing to do on each occasion is to call those circles consciously again, and formally dismiss them with a brief thought of thanks and goodwill. Perhaps this single dismissive couplet will accomplish the whole process: *"Farewell my thought-folk, bless you all, but please return when next I call."*

It might be objected that such words are not very magical or impressively mysterious, but those elements are indeed present in their significance and also in their correct cadence of pronounciation. There is really no need for words at all, but since we humans are accustomed to using them for framing our intentions, that is the main reason for their employment here. A child does not communicate with its mother by words, but by bodily movements, facial expressions, gestures, and significant sounds. When in the womb, it communicates purely by chemical changes. For example, if it needs some special element, the fetus signals its mother to eat or drink whatever contains that requirement, and she usually manages to get the message. The unborn child and its mother have a considerable understanding between them, and a great deal more intelligent contact can be established with people while they are still in their mothers' wombs than might be supposed. Some attempts have indeed been made at educating the unborn with quite surprising results, especially in cases where the fetuses in question were females.

With earlier generations it was the custom to educate the sexes separately because of physical differences, and the two entirely opposite types of training were given, even to providing schools in which boys and girls attended separate classes. This almost inevitably resulted in homosexuality among the boys and a preoccupation with sexual subjects among the girls. It became a known thing amongst young males that if a girl with unusual interests in sex was being sought, the best place to look for her would be amid a group of convent-taught teenagers. With all the heavy emphasis that was placed on sex as a sinful and repulsive subject, it was no wonder they found it such a fascinating and attractive topic. Hidden behind barriers of hints and mysterious warnings of unmentionable woes coming to those who ignored them, the girls could do little else than become obsessed with such strangely interesting stories. The euphemistic language used to avoid reference to direct sexual subjects did not help either. A case is known of a girl who was convinced that self-abuse literally meant swearing at herself in a mirror!

Today's children are far more fortunate. Educationalists are reaching the sensible conclusion that young males and females are best taught together. Their bodies are no longer made mysterious to each other, and their minds are expected to tackle the same problems. Even their erstwhile special skills are encouraged to be interchangeable. For example, a male is expected to be able to bathe and change a baby, while a female should be able to change a tire or a tap washer. Although a man cannot yet actually *have* his baby, he is encouraged to be present at its birth and assist by cutting the umbilical cord, and such small services that make him feel he is partaking in the process somehow. From a social and material standpoint, men and women have become more equal in this century than in any other. They took the first step by regarding their deities as beings of both sexes quite apart from themselves, who caused happenings to humanity by intending them.

It is mostly in the area of cultural, social, and religious affairs that women have exerted their most significant influence. Prior to Christianity there were many beautiful and well-served temples devoted to the greatest Goddess ideal under all kinds of names and titles scattered throughout the civilized world. As we have already noted, women were running their own types of religious rites exclusively of males many centuries ago (to the evident disapproval of masculine deities), even if it were a family affair such as noted in Jeremiah 7:18: "Children gather the wood and fathers kindle the fire, and the women knead their dough to make cakes for the queen of heaven and pour out drink offerings unto other gods that they may provoke me to anger." Inciting Yahweh into his frequent bouts of ill temper was scarcely a motive suggested by subsequent remarks attributed to the Jewish women of Pathros in Egypt further along in Chapter 44, verse 19: "And when we burned incense to the queen of heaven and poured out drink offerings to her, did we make cake-offerings to her without our men." It is believed those early cake-offerings have descended to us at this very time in the shape of the well-known hot-cross buns, which commemorate the sacrifice of our titular Sacred King, Jesus Christ.

Those were called in Greek *bouns*, from *bous*, an ox, since they were marked with the sign of horns and were intended as a substitute for the sacrifice of that animal at temple altars. They were mostly made from fine flour and honey, and were always the appropriate offering at the temple of Athena at Athens. That custom was said to have begun with Cecrops, the original founder of that settlement, in about 1550 B.C. He was a native of Saïs in Egypt, where the temples of Isis were already familiar with the solar-crossed sacrificial cakes, of which the horn-marked variety were obviously an appropriate lunar example. In fact the eventual substitution of bread for the Victim's body, and wine for his blood, was in all probability a feminine idea adopted when the majority of women could no longer tolerate the thought of cutting up and cooking a sacrificed fellow human, however willing he or she might have been to take the principal part in such a performance. First animals became surrogates, and later on vegetable products took over from them. It would be interesting to see if some ultimate form of mineral might eventually replace the vegetable oblation in our religious ceremonies, and to speculate on the method used to symbolize it. That would naturally depend on how we develop our sense of Deism and whether we can ever learn to *live it* as an expression of Existence Itself—a combination of consciousness blending both complementary polarities of power into ONE BLESSED BEING Who will be far above and beyond anything that either sex could possibly become by itself. That would mean the consummation of our truly Mystical Marriage had taken place at last, and both Man and Woman would become GOD IS (Goddess) in each other forevermore.

Sculpture based on primitive Goddess

Chapter Five

Our Mystical Mother

Why should so many mortals begin believing in some kind of a deity and eventually end their lives with little or no beliefs in any such being? The simple answer, of course, is disillusionment. Their earliest beliefs, probably imparted by their parents, did not match their own experience of life, hence the discrepancy between their two states of selfhood. So we must be careful not to make a Mother-ideal that can be discredited easily enough by ordinary mortals because it seems too improbable or unsatisfactory. Probably the reason the old gods lasted so long was that they were seen as being full of human idiosyncrasies themselves, and were believed to be superior only because of their spiritual structure or reputed power to aid us if we pleaded with them properly. In those days an approach to the Gods was assumed to be a matter of know-how. If you knew the right words and techniques, they would respond as requested, but otherwise you would only be wasting your time. The problem was principally that each God or Goddess called for a particular type of approach that encouraged it to bestow favors, and each had its special sacrificial needs that had to be satisfied in order to attract attention. It was almost as if the Gods were demanding a set fee for professional services just like any other sort of specialist.

With the Judeo-Christian ideal of Deity, which most modern mortals are assumed to accept in principle, it is generally believed that adherence to a code of conduct will qualify an approaching human for favorable attention, while contrary behavior will call for retributory or corrective reprisals. That is more or less the notion of karma expressed in another form, or put in a different way, Severity tempered with Mercy, resulting in Justice. With pure Judaism, of course, a human element is not considered possible in Deity, whereas with Christianity such is seen as an essential, as personified in Jesus—who once lived like a predecessor, Osiris, on this Earth, who was likewise slain by political enemies, and who consequently continues to exist in a Heaven-state where he remains to help human adherents. It is simply another version of the Sacred King story, which is common to so many cultures. The feminine aspect attached to Osiris, however, was his sister-wife Isis, while with Jesus it became his mother Miriam, a name which signifies the sea, reputed to be the most ancient Mother of all humankind. Since she acted as an agent for the feminine Holy Spirit on Earth, she would certainly serve as a human symbol for our idealized modern Magna Mater if such were acceptable to Christians, which at present it is not, so the idea must remain as people are best able to appreciate it. Hence the scheme of everyone selecting their own idealized visual symbol. There seems to be no objections to artistic impressions of the Mary-image, if such should be a genuine desire, but it seems preferable that people ought to pick a noncontroversial picture, and the Mary-image is already associated in so many minds with an entirely contradictory ideology. Besides, the concept of Mary in person as being representative of a divine aspect is abhorrent to a large proportion of people who would otherwise accept an unpersonified principle.

To such persons, and to whoever else might prefer the presentation, our feminine aspect of Deity might be more acceptable as a visual symbol as presented in Figure 1. This could be described as a Quarternity emblem depicting crossed ovals, one of which represents the mouth and the other a vagina, with supporting symbolism to match. The central sign is that of four sperm cells superimposed on each other to indicate multiple possibilities of paternity, and it also shows itself as a swastika, a very old sign of virility and active power. Sometimes this is called the Hammer of Thor, which was a euphemism for the phallus of the Thunder God because of motions made during a sex act being likened to those of a hammer in action. The numerous dots included in the framework of the design represent the innumerable humans deriving from the Goddess herself, and the surrounding motto of *Magna Mater memorare me* means exactly what it says: "Great Mother remember me." It conveys a hope held by the viewer that the Deity will indeed maintain a conscious relationship with him or her.

Simple though it may look, this entire glyph has a

lot more meaning than might appear on its surface. In former times its principle was shown by the Shielah na Gig, a grossly distorted fertility figure, sometimes bent over backwards with head between her legs so as to place a grinning mouth in close proximity to her vagina, held apart at the edges with the fingertips of both hands. This presented the man-feared *vagina dentata*, or toothed vagina, threatening to bite the penis from unwelcome male entrants. A choice of two holes was being offered—one being a correct and fertile prefer-

Figure 1 — The Bloodmother Symbol

ence, while the other is nonproductive and dangerous. There is a possibility that since the Shielah na Gig is a predominantly Celtic figure, it may be the origin of the typically British saying of "top-hole," in the sense of anything that is done especially well or is the very best of its kind. More usually though, the Shielah was shown with her head in the upright position but still with wide mouth and extended vulva.

An interesting point is that her name probably connects with the Latin *gigno*—to beget, to bring forth, to produce—in the sense of her being an emblem of the Mother whence everything came from. Crude as she may seem to cultivated people, a simple portrayal of a plain sex-fact may be much more meaningful than a shelfful of sermons. It might be well to remember that in later and more artistic periods the Virgin was depicted as having a vaginal-shaped aura around herself, and as being usually clothed in blue and white, such being the colors of the Temple Veil, which was normally woven by virginal young women and which was said to have been rent in two during the death of Jesus on the cross. The rending of the veil was said to have symbolized the division between the Old and the New Dispensations. Blue and white are now the colors of Israel as a sovereign state, while its central design, so often described as the "Shield of David," is the hexagrammoid interlacing of two triangles. Apart from this being a reef knot, the female pudenda was often represented by a triangle with the point down, or a lozenge which is two triangles joined base to base. If those are pushed together by the points, they will make a perfect Shield of David shape, thus disclosing its feminine derivation. It might also be noted that Mary's connection with the Blood-Royal was said to be via the House of David.

For those able to find significance in sonic values, it should be noted that the three letters of the Hebrew alphabet classified as "mothers" are *A, M,* and *Sh.* Those are all natural sounds that mothers have made to their babies since time immemorial—the alerting or warning "Ah-ah," the comforting and companionable "MMMMMMM," and the soothing or slumberous "SSSSSHHHH"—all associated with the sea and the cycle of life connected with waking a baby up, cuddling it, and putting it to sleep again. "Mum" is usually the first sensible sound a baby makes, so it is scarcely surprising that it means "mother" in so many languages. The Semitic version is Amah or Umm, and the reverence attached to the sonic OMM in Sanskrit, reputed to be a root-language of so many humans, is well known by those who may not know its matriarchal meaning consciously. We instinctively pay honor to our greatest Mother every time we use the familiar word *amen.* However far we may grow away from her womb physically, we return to it mentally on more occasions than are generally recognized.

What else are our houses, dwellings, or shelters of any kind except womb substitutes? What else is sleep except a temporary death, and how otherwise could we exist without a sojourn in Mother Earth, from whose womb so many mortals believe we shall eventually return in due course? What else are motor cars except mobile womb-symbols that move us from one point to another? If it comes to this sort of symbology, any kind of vehicle ever invented is an alternative womb in which many of us may travel together for some common purpose. In effect an aircraft or a ship is a type of womb in which we are borne to the very ends of our Earth, and so can the spacecraft be considered that will bear our species to some other planet altogether. It is interesting to think that our first traveling womb was a ship or craft of some kind which bore us on the breast of our oldest Mother, the ocean. From first to last our Mother carries us in one form or another. The womb symbology of containers, coverings, or wrappings of almost any kind has long been recognized as such by psychologists of every school.

From the first time that humans crawled into a cave and covered themselves with animal skins, to the present period, when people can retire into the most luxurious conditions possible, a bed has always been considered the basic object around which a home gets built, and a bed is unquestionably a mother symbol, since it is so womblike. That is possibly the reason that waterbeds have become our latest luxury, on account of the fact that their tactile feel is so reminiscent of the amniotic fluid in which we spent those first few months of our present personalities. One way or another, mother substitutes have become a human necessity without which our world would be unbearable for most of us, and so we need to think of or invent them in whatever practical ways we can imagine, which applies to spiritual levels of life even more than physical ones.

That is why it is so important that we should formulate satisfactory relationships with our feminine Deity, because if we do not, our lives will become badly imbalanced and short of real meaning. Most humans will seek her subconsciously through the symbolic substitutes they encounter in everyday living, such as female human friends and relatives, or the more material objects like those previously mentioned— perhaps a warm bath, because this is really a comfortable container filled with warmly welcoming water, like the original wombs in which we were once happy. In fact one of the worst experiences a human can possibly have is to survive an attempted abortion while in the last stage of pregnancy, especially if it is attempted by physical interference, such as by the insertion of a knitting needle.

Rejection by other humans for any reason is always a character-changing and unpleasant experience to undergo, whether a very trivial rejection or one of much more marked degree. Rejection by one's own mother from her womb, however, particularly if attempted by mechanical means, is undoubtedly the ultimate rejection any human being could undergo. It is unfortunate that we cannot obtain accurate information concerning those who murdered their mothers or treated them very badly in later life, to find out whether early attempts had been made to abort them. Studies along such lines might produce some really valuable information. Bad behavior patterns can very easily be implanted during the earliest periods of our materialization in the maternal womb because of the interference with normal processes of nature, and intrusions of foreign bodies are unmistakable evidence of being unwanted. Mothers are not likely to be popular people with those surviving such an unwelcome shock, and that possibility should always be considered by anyone studying human characteristics. Similar interest might also be taken in the cases of those that have managed to achieve success in their lives despite the presence of an IUD in their mothers' wombs.

With our idealized Mother concept, however, there is no danger of rejection, because she must always be the sort of Mother that anyone would want to have if that were really possible. Nevertheless, she must certainly not be thought of as a Mother who did not correct her children's conduct whenever that might be necessary, although she would never do this in a foolish manner or without exercising a maximum of wisdom. Her reaction to bad behavior would always be intelligently calculated to be the most appropriate response to whatever behavior was in question. That means to say, her children would have to understand that they themselves had caused her reactions as a direct result of their own behavior, and if they did not like what was happening, then they had only themselves to blame and could stop it as soon as they changed their conduct. Somehow they must be made to see that they were always afforded opportunities to alter their situations, and it has to be made perfectly plain to them that the option will always be theirs.

Charles Kingsley put this very well in his famous "Water Babies," with his two opposite female sister-figures—an indulgent Mrs. Do-as-you-would-be-done-by, and her strict sister Mrs. Be-done-by-as-you-did, who checked the children's conduct and punished them for bad behavior, though always with perfect justice and genuine regret for the necessity of doing so.

Anyone who has not read this famous tale should definitely do so for the sake of its esoteric significance, especially its maternal symbology, which is particularly applicable to our Mystical Mother concept. Kingsley's description of a Universal Mother at the end—who never moved physically yet created everything continually from her own mind and consciousness—was a wonderfully imaginative piece of prose. Perhaps the most surprising thing connected with the story was its author's profession as an Anglican clergyman. Somehow one does not generally associate Establishment clergy with such unusual thinking. He was very careful to point out in his fable that when the time came when no child would ever need punishing again, the hideous Mrs. Be-done-by-as-you-did would become as beautiful as her twin sister again, and everyone would live happily forever afterwards.

This happy-ever-afterwards theme of hope has inspired every human search for an ideal of anything ever since we began looking for whatever it might be, even if this were a Quest for a Quest or a search for what to seek for. Few situations are more frustrating than not knowing what to do, where to go, or even which objective to pursue. Once an objective can be clearly defined and strongly enough desired, the complete picture changes and we become altogether different people. Although most humans' main motive in life is to make money, that is scarcely a very satisfying substitute for more spiritual and much deeper drives linked with living. Once we know for certain what we want, the next step is to know how to get it, and then the whens and wheres will come as circumstances allow. Most of all, we need to know *why* anything should be worth expending energy to gain.

At least we should know by now that our objective is to find an acceptable feminine aspect of Deity in order to counterbalance the ever-masculine aspect we have been worshipping in the West for far too long. That is the what. The why is so that the two may be eventually mated in our minds, thus leading toward the perfection of our human species. The when is naturally unknown but needed as soon as practically possible. The where is wherever this concept may be required to correct the course of our Western civilization. The how is by whatever means may seem adequate or practical pursuant to the achievement of our original intention. Even those addicted to literal beliefs in Biblical scriptures can scarcely avoid the implications of Genesis 1:27: "So God created man in his own image. In the image of God created he him. Male and female created he them." It is only in the next chapter that the creation of Adam from earthly elements and the subsequent production of Eve is mentioned. Those apparently separate creations are sometimes taken to mean that the Deity imagined or created the idea of humanity in Its consciousness before bringing us to life as earthly beings. If so, then Deity saw Itself as being both male and female, as a single entity of which we are a reflected duplicate or a materialized projection, whichever way we might prefer to view ourselves. Since the very next verse goes on to say, "And God blessed them and said unto them be fruitful and multiply," it would appear that the Deity regarded Its creations as prolific people. Furthermore it was not those initial "images" that were forbidden to eat the fruit from the Tree of Knowledge in the Garden of Eden, but the Earth-made man Adam and his cloned female partner Eve. Whatever conclusions may be reached from this, it is certain that the early writers of scripture believed in the biology of their God even if they knew very little about their own.

Gods were always paired in early eras, and a suitable mate was found for each according to its nature. When monotheism first arose, the Deity was mainly of a predominantly male nature, or else was far above both human genders and therefore needed nothing to complete its spiritual state. Now we are being asked to link all three conditions together as a composite concept of Deity, as idealized by male-female Principles expressing themselves conjunctly as a unified Entity. Nevertheless we are here concentrating on the female Principle in particular, because this has been sadly neglected in our past by most Westerners, and we now need to reenergize it by building it up again with fresh thinking and attention. Nevertheless, the feminine polarity strength must never be allowed to exceed its masculine counterpart so far as pure effect is concerned. Without such paternal potency, a Mother of any sort simply could not exist in the first place. The mere fact of Motherhood automatically implies a fertile male to make her so. We are not yet a self-fertilizing species of creature. So with every act of attention paid to our Mother principle, a brief acknowledgment should be included to the Father-force behind our beings.

Seeing that the act of male fertilization is only a

matter of moments in contrast with the nine-month long pregnancy needed to gestate the resultant child, it would seem appropriate that any Father-acknowledgment should be short and very intense, while the Mother-equivalent ought to be a great deal longer and a lot more detailed. This seems to make much better symbology, and if we propose to use symbols as a means of contacting the Energy we believe to be our Primal Parents, they might as well be satisfactory ones. Take for example the Christian custom of crossing oneself. A manual gesture of touching the forehead, breast, and shoulders while saying or thinking, "In the name of the Father, and of the Son, and of the Holy Spirit, amen." How many of those Christian millions who make the movement without thinking about it realize that they have made an act of spiritual sex? The vertical movement represents the phallic penetration of the horizontal vaginal one. Moreover, the accompanying thinking should formulate the male principle of the Father and Son from top to bottom, while the female principle is indicated by the side-to-side motion and the words "And of the Holy Spirit amen," the operative word being *amen*, which as we have seen is purely feminine. Although it might surprise or possibly shock some Christians to discover the deeper meaning behind a familiar formula, such an interpretation ought only to make this majority appreciate it a great deal more and treat it with the reverence it truly deserves. As an item of further significance, the Eastern Orthodox Church directs its crossing from right to left shoulder, while the Western Church does theirs in the opposite direction, from left to right. So the former ends on a feminine emphasis, and the latter chooses a masculine one.

The reason for this association of right with masculine and left with feminine is extremely simple. With a male the right hand is normally the weapon-carrying one, but with a female her left arm is the baby-bearer, as she carries it close to her left breast. It was normal for a male to keep his female on his left side in case he needed to use his right arm in her defense. Many millennia later this became the custom of always walking so that a female companion was closest to the wall in public places, or offering one's left arm to a lady for her support. In that way she could cling tightly if need be without interfering with her man's mobility. The right-male and left-female linkage is an extremely ancient one in our human heritage, and very unlikely to vanish entirely after only a few generations. Our instincts are only ancestral memories implanted in our genes that have become inoperative on conscious levels yet are still capable of putting pressures on us from far deeper driving points.

The only reason for associating good with a right-hand path and evil with a left-hand one is that the former was taken to be the solar course of day and light, whereas its opposite was presumed to be that of lunar night and darkness, when it became much easier to work wickedness, such as surprise attacks, robberies, ambushes, or other malicious moves. Most olden temples were oriented on an east-west axis so that one faced the Sun as it arose in the east, appeared to travel overhead, then sank in the west where it continued to go through the Underworld until rising again next morning. Christians always placed their sanctuaries in the east, since they regarded Jesus as "the Sun of Righteousness," and consequently pointed their worship in that direction. The Archangel Michael too, who is termed Leader of the Hosts of Light, was always considered as being at the right hand of God, while the Supreme Being Itself was represented as the crowned head of an elder shown in right-sided profile to make it quite clear that no evil could possibly exist in such a holy head.

This right-good left-evil idea became so deeply fixed in people's minds that with all dramas the evil characters traditionally entered from the left or "sinister" side of the stage and were dark like the night, while the good ones entered from the right and were fair like the day. God characters were supposed to descend from above by some device made to resemble an assumed agency of celestial transport, hence the saying, *Deus ex machina,* or "the God out of the machine." In fact, so firmly embedded in most people's minds did the left-bad right-good association become that it still persists genetically today, though scarcely to the same extent as formerly. At one time a visitor was expected to enter a home right foot first to indicate good intentions, and the New Year custom of "first footing" is still kept up to this day, mainly in Scotland.

Once an idea becomes an integral part of a particular people's awareness of themselves, it becomes easier to adapt it than eliminate it. That was well known to early Christians attempting to replace Pagan faiths and customs with their own reformed ideology. As a rule they simply offered more acceptable substitutes for former practices or retained the practice in an altered form with a parallel significance. Even so, it was not until they reintroduced the Mother Deity concept in a greatly reduced role as the Virgin Mary that the Church really got a grip on the majority of Western civilization at that period. Eventually, as history shows, the predominantly masculine power in the Church prevailed, and the Virgin Mother concept became reduced in rank to mere sainthood, and subsequently to a status of almost total insignificance, by the most belligerent and anti-mystical congregations claiming connections with Christianity (although they had much more in common with the principles of extreme Judaism or even Islam than with any sort of genuine Christianity). Such firm rejecters of the feminine principle in Deity can be encountered in fundamentalism today. They provide as puzzling an example as those ultra-feminists who would eliminate all ideas of masculinity from any connected with the Creative Consciousness. How they suppose they came to this world themselves without a masculine agency, or what they would be like if every masculine characteristic were removed from them, Heaven alone knows.

Although parthenogenesis, or an apparently virgin birth, is physiologically possible, it is not only exceptionally rare but the fetus borne by the female in question is always that of her twin sister—it is a split egg that was fertilized by her father at the same time as herself. However, since it had incorporated itself inside her anatomy, it would have to wait until her body produced the hormones needed for finishing its finalized form. So far as may be known, only a single instance of a male bearing his own brother inside himself has been recorded. This resulted in the death of the older boy, on whom a post mortem was performed in the 18th century, and the whole phenomenon was preserved in spirits at a medical museum in London. Unfortunately, it was destroyed by enemy bombing during the Second World War.

For many centuries it has been a magical dream to create an artificial man called an homunculus, and all sorts of methods have been proposed to accomplish this. Paracelsus suggested keeping a phial of human sperm warm in decaying dung to generate heat for 40 days, at the end of which a transparent outline of a miniature human should be seen. After that the creature had to be nourished on the arcanum of human blood, then it would slowly materialize and become a solid body capable of learning and communicating with its creator. An homunculus, however, would always remain a mini-mortal and live permanently in its bottle while being blood-fed with this mysterious arcanum, which Paracelsus did not leave any formula for making. What is interesting is the *idea* of creating a child outside of a human womb, which goes as far back as the sixteenth century. It has only become a practical possibility in our times, when the egg from one woman can be fertilized with the seed of a man she has never met and then gestated in the womb of a woman unknown to either. It is believed that experiments are being made to discover the possibilities of breeding humans in the wombs of other animals. Genetic engineering may be a fascinating science, but it opens up very dangerous knowledge, none of which would ever have been possible without the initial ideas that started the train of consciousness responsible for results in this world.

How should we humans bring our ideas to birth as actualities? Oldtime Qabbalists postulated a process that is the metaphysical equivalent of the same system by which we ourselves became incarnate. This process could be called an act of spiritual sex between ourselves and the Supreme Being, who was considered to be the single source of consciousness per se. They saw it as being a gradual affair, commencing with a universal condition of Nothingness before anything exists at all, and even that was considered to consist of three stages: (1) No-thing, (2) Nothing and Infinity, or Empty Endlessness, and (3) Nothing, Infinity, and Light. At this point the possibility of Something arises. They classified this as Zero, the point where every possibility begins. In itself it is the implication of indefinite enumerations to follow. The next stage was termed Origins, or where everything begins to be something by thinking about it. We might call it a condition of thinking about thought. From a sexual viewpoint, it would be the initial attraction that draws people of complementary polarities together and suggests closer congress. Following that came the stage of Creation, which is an equivalent of the sex act itself, when masculine and feminine principles come together and unite in ultimate enjoyment of each other. Afterwards came the much slower but entirely necessary period of Formation, which amounts to gestation in the womb, or being put together carefully so as to make an eventual entity or Whole out of the many items associating with each other. Last of all of course came the time of Expression, or the birth and bringing-up stage during which the emergent entity becomes a being in its own right and is capable of assuming responsibility for its own behavior.

This is why the Hebrews ideally saw themselves as all being feminine in relation to their masculine Deity concept. Just as they could breed physical children amongst themselves by means of ordinary biological sex, so might they breed ideas and concepts by metaphysical sex with their Deity. Hence most of them believed in a Father figure who would reach into the Nothing with them, and together they would generate the germ of an idea, which they would then gestate until it could be brought forth and developed as an independent creation of consciousness causing benefits to everyone concerned. True, they had their mystical Mother, in exile from Heaven, as the Shekinah amongst them on Earth, but she was regarded as a divine vehicle for their God to dwell in while visiting his chosen people, and she would return from whence she came when the last mortal might be fit enough to accompany her.

Consider the curious example of Israel in our modern world. Who could imagine them making war on themselves to a degree of desperate destruction? Such a situation would be unbelievable. They might disagree with each other on many issues and quarrel ceaselessly concerning matters that to others might seem pointless or insignificant, but to contemplate deliberate mass murder of each other in an all-out war would be totally unthinkable. The interesting point is why that should be so.

The fact is that every authentic Israeli is brought up to believe that all other Israelis and Jews, no matter how many or how distant, are blood relations of theirs in the same spiritual family and are therefore especially sacred as such. Though they may not think much of each other as individuals, even hating members of their own race as bitterly as any human might ever do, they will always regard themselves as being parts of the same family, bonded by a blood that they believe in with every fiber of their beings. They might not believe in any kind of a Deity or practice any particular type of religion, and in fact many of the kibbutzim are agnostic or even atheist, but all are completely and entirely dedicated to an identical belief in themselves and their purpose as a people because of their shared blood. If they regard this blood as being a matriarchal principle, then they are accepting it as a symbol of common Motherhood, and if we are ever to believe sincerely in the Brotherhood of Man ideal, then we shall have to conceive a common Mother as an ideal in whom we might all feel united—first from a racial and then from a purely human angle. If the Israelis can do this for themselves as one single section of that humanity, why should it not be possible to extend the same principle so as to cover the entire mass of humankind all over the world?

Such indeed has been the dream of many human beings since a very early era, but few have ever been able to make it work as a practical proposition, owing to almost inevitable clashes of ideology and political problems. However, with the relatively recent rise of feminism and the actual participation of women in fields of action hitherto regarded as exclusively male areas, there could be hope for the establishment of a common Mother concept that includes everyone on Earth. How we could all consider ourselves as genuine brothers and sisters without acknowledging some mythical Mother figure is an unanswerable question. Exactly how we see her is a matter for everyone to decide for themselves, but that we should all recognize the same Idea or Principle *together* is essential for the sake of ourselves and our world, if not for other worlds than this one eventually.

What we have to do is conceive the ideal of a Mother mutually acceptable to the whole of humanity and relate with it so potently that we would regard ourselves as a family bound together by the strongest ties believable—those of blood itself. The fact that these bonds are more spiritual than physical should only serve to strengthen rather than weaken them, since what is material can only last for as long as its lifetime on Earth. That may not be very long in the case of the average mortal, but so far as spiritual beliefs are concerned, it might be many millennia. Christianity has existed for virtually 2,000 years, and other religions a lot longer. Judaism alone is three times as long. Seeing that our beliefs outlast us so considerably, they might as well be given the respect they deserve.

For those who cannot accept the ideal of any Deity whatever, it should still be possible to conceive a suitable type of Mother for the whole of humanity to share, and make whatever mental relationships with this they please. If they cannot accept the Bloodmother symbol suggested, then let them design their own if they can, or choose whatever they prefer to represent the principle of femininity in a favorable light. If they have any serious difficulties with formulating definite ideas, it would be a good notion to start by asking, What sort of woman would my ideal Mother be? and divide the inquiry into categories, such as

1. Race or nationality? Coloring—dark, fair, or medium?
2. Temperament? Age and appearance? Height and size?
3. Religious inclinations?
4. Political affiliations?
5. Employment—professional or vocational?
6. Education? Recreational interests?
7. Vocal qualities—any particular attributes?
8. Sexual attitudes—sympathies and antipathies?
9. What would I admire most in her? Desire least?

Then continue asking questions of that type until satisfied with the answers. Something definite should appear after a series of such queries.

Once some clear ideas concerning an ideal Mother have been obtained, the next thing to find out is what she would want the inquirer to do if she were a real person, which in a sense she is, being a personification of that individual's ideas concerning motherhood. Our own earthly parents are very seldom the people we think they are, but mostly characters composed of our ideas about them. Once they are dead, we remember them not exactly as they really were, but as we thought they seemed. What we are really looking at is our own beliefs and memories of them. Therefore whatever notions or ideas we may hold concerning a mystical Mother of Mankind or a Blessed Bloodbeing are neither more nor less valid than those based on living people who are or were our own closest relatives. The ideas concerning that mystical Mother are highly unlikely to have a worse effect on us than those we already hold about our parents, and they could indeed prove much better, since we would naturally see our ideal Mother in the best possible light.

As soon as a sense of contact with our Bloodmother can be depended on, it should be strengthened and built up by a variety of small intentional thinkings based on the "Brother Lawrence" technique, which means involving her with one's daily life in the most commonplace matters. Brother Lawrence, a seventeenth century Carmelite monk of Alsatian origins, was domiciled in a Parisian house of that Order and worked for some time as a cook in the community. He became well known for his "Practice of the Presence of God," or treating his Deity with the greatest of familiarity, as if It were an intimate friend present among the commonest kitchen conditions just as much as if those were the most splendid sanctuary. Lawrence was equally happy with either. For him, God became his perfect lifelong companion and confidant with whom he could communicate at any time and any place. He would laugh and joke with his Deity as though It were sitting beside him, and would mention quite trivial matters in almost the same breath as serious subjects. Today of course he would be classed as some kind of pathological fantasist, unable to distinguish between rubbish and reality. More and more, however, the most modern psychiatrists are beginning to realize the vital necessity of mentally manufactured mythology in our lives, providing this fulfills an essential function and is kept under careful control. The ill effects of deliberate dream deprival are now very well known, and children are instinctive mythmakers because they know within themselves that they need to be in order to adapt to a life that is becoming more menacing at every turn. So which myths are preferable? Those concerning a beautiful and beneficent God-Being, or the alternatives offered by horror comics and video nasties? There can scarcely be much argument on that point. Maybe moderns might prefer to think of Brother Lawrence as a perpetual child, but the truth is that he lived a very long and happy life, was greatly loved by everyone who knew him, and died a peaceful and comfortable death surrounded by kindness and beneficence. If such is the result of one man's mythmaking, then may we all be mythmakers.

Besides, as we have seen, a myth does not mean an intentional falsehood intended to injure anyone. It means an underlying truth presented in such a way that it catches the imagination, helps hearers to understand, is easy to remember, and only brings benefits to all concerned. A myth exists only in the method or form by which that decorated truth is presented to us for familiarization. Our Bloodbeing is certainly no myth so far as its existence goes. How can it possibly be untrue if it amounts to our ancestry, our genetics, and whatever we have inherited from our past or intend to circulate through our consciousness for the benefit of future folk? If our mythical Bloodmother consists of all that is or has been good in every mother who has lived or ever will live in our human world, who would be stupid enough to say that such a concept has no reality or significance worth bothering with? We might just as well deny our own existence, or else claim that human-kind itself is the greatest myth ever invented by an ingenious imagination. Maybe we are, after all, but before we give ourselves up for lost, let us first see not only what we can do with our Bloodmother but also what she can do for us.

Head of Demeter with her attributes:
sheaves of corn, poppies and snakes

Chapter Six

Concept
Creation

The creation of a Mother concept should not present any serious problems for the average person of normal intelligence who is prepared to spend sufficient time and effort in doing so. What becomes a lot more difficult is believing in it strongly enough to make its influence known and perceptible in the areas of our ordinary lives and courses of consciousness. That is to say, can a concept by itself have enough power to modify human behavior by our beliefs in it? There is no doubt that it can if we think about the conduct that results from people's belief in a God concept or whatever Power they assume is superior to themselves. We have only to look at what political terrorists will do for the sake of the "cause" they support to see the effects of ideal-beliefs on some human beings. Therefore, working on the assumption that we *can* make myths that would improve the quality of our lives, and that would bring us blessings and benefits if we use them properly, let us see what can be done with the concept of our Blood-mother once she is contacted and condensed as Brother

Lawrence suggested.

First we will need to bring her into our lives by thinking of her often in connection with ordinary, trivial, and even the most intimate occasions. Does any normal small child object to its mother's presence while being bathed or on the toilet? Could any reasonable mother be offended by her child's bodily behavior? She might be worried or concerned if there were any cause for alarm, but she would certainly not be bothered or shocked without some very sound and adequate reason. Therefore the presence of a beneficent and totally sympathetic maternal influence should be a perfectly natural and normal one to suppose, even if invisible or imperceptible to ordinary physical senses. We might be well aware that we are creating a Mother concept out of our own consciousness, but at the same time we should realize equally well that we are really making a vehicle for the reality to occupy when it is ready. Our thoughts may make the body, but the soul and Spirit will animate it from elsewhere, and that will constitute the reality which in time will respond to and answer our attentive awareness. We might say we are making a mental *machina* for our *Deus* to descend to Earth with.

We give identity to things and people or even pet animals by donating proper names, without which we would not admit identity at all. Since we need to emphasize our concept's reality in every way we can, we each should settle for a suitable name that we have decided upon ourselves. Perhaps Christians might prefer to choose Mary, or Pagans Diana, for example. It would be perfectly permissible to invent a name-word if such were descriptive and reasonable. Above all, it must be and feel entirely appropriate and completely comfortable, which means it should be brief and familiar in usage. If there should be real difficulty in finding a suitable name, it would be quite reasonable to select a temporary substitute, if this were acceptable to all concerned.

For example, if we look up the Greek word for "mother," we shall find *meter*, nearly the same as the Latin *mater*. So the literal meaning of *Demeter* is "people mother," because *demos* means "people" in Greek. Although we may be quite correct in thinking of a Mother concept as Demeter, it scarcely seems appropriate for a modern mortal; but if we consider a "Me" idea and make MEMAME (pronounced in three syllables—ME-MA-ME), we should have quite a pleasing word not at all dissimilar to the familiar "mum" or "mummie" so widely used by juvenile English speakers. So as a cover name for our present purposes, let us settle for MEMAME, at least as a temporary name for the ideal matriarchal concept we are in the process of constructing.

MEMAME is to be considered present with the help of imagination whenever we call her for conscious company. Just as Brother Lawrence considered his God present while he was handling his pots and pans, so may we believe MEMAME to be sharing an interest in similar activities. For example, if anyone intended to go for a walk in the countryside, he or she might think: "MEMAME, I'm going for a walk to be with Nature for a while, so why not come with me and see everything through my eyes and mind? If you can suggest some interesting ideas to me, I'll welcome them, so please come along." Or if watching a TV or video, invite MEMAME to share it and offer her views and opinions. However, be careful to ask her only if her presence is directly needed for some particular reason, and never under any circumstances call her for idle or absurd purposes. If she is required to behave towards us as we would have her act if she were physically real, then we will have to behave in a reciprocal fashion towards her, using the same sort of language, gestures, and words as if our mortal mothers were with us as idealized people. Should there be any particular topics or types of behavior we know would be annoying or offensive to them, then we should avoid expressing ourselves in those ways while conscious of our Concept's company. The general rule of conduct is to behave exactly as if in the physical presence of a human personage of equal significance. This is very important, since it means that control factors are being intentionally applied as required, which is essential to all well-motivated magic.

So far as males are concerned, there are several bodily postures that may be presented so as to show sympathy with the feminine aspect being approached. One is the "pregnancy-protective" attitude, which is demonstrated by interlinking the fingers of both hands and pressing the palms to the lower abdomen. This means, "I am gestating an idea, may it come to something really significant in due course." Another is the breast-guard in which the arms are crossed right over left with the palms of the hands pressing on alternate breasts. This usually signifies, "Let nothing harmful come to anyone from the ideology I have to offer." Also there is the breast offering position wherein the thumb and forefinger of one hand is placed closely beneath the opposite breast while the forearm on that side is extended in friendly fashion with the palm upwards as if to say, "Here is something I feel you ought to have." With the left breast that would be an intention of merciful kindness, and with the right one, an offering of careful discipline. This arrangement would align with the ideas on the Tree of Life, which naturally reverses humans identifying themselves with it, as in a mirror image.

One great advantage of belonging to an orthodox faith of any kind is that it usually has very well thought out, ready-made prayer formulae that are easily re-membered and applicable to almost any situation. The Roman section of the Christian Church has a great number of these, and one of the most popular is the "Hail Mary," or special salutation to the Virgin Mother, which says very simply and succinctly: "Hail Mary, full of grace, the Lord is with thee. Blessed art thou amongst women and blessed is the fruit of thy womb Jesus. Holy Mary, Mother of God, pray for us sinners now and at the hour of our death, Amen." The first part of the prayer is a scriptural quote presumed to have been made by the Archangel Gabriel announcing her preg-nancy, and the second, a pious hope by her petitioners for her attention at the greatest hour of human need. It is especially interesting to note the connection made between the birth of an Avatar and our own deaths, which he was supposed to sanctify by his sacrifice of life. Since this lovely little prayer can scarcely be improved on so far as format or meter is concerned, we feel quite justified in adapting it for present purposes:

"Hail Lady of all life and matrix of humankind, our loving thoughts are always with thee. Be with us blessed Bloodmother on this our Earth to counsel, chasten, and console us till we meet once more together in thy wondrous womb, amen."

Of for those special few seeking even deeper significance:

"Beloved Bloodmother of my especial breed, welcome me this magic moment with your wondrous womb. Let me learn to live in love with all you are so that my seeking spirit serves the Sangreal."

Furthermore, just as there is a formulary of Christian faith, such as the Nicene Creed, which proves very useful when reviewing the various fundamental beliefs that comprise it, so should there be a comparable overview of what has been propounded in our present pages. This could be concerted as:

"I believe in life that comes of love made manifest between our Lord thereof and his coequal consort our Bloodmother. Moreover I believe this has both point and purpose for us to pursue with faith in its fulfillment till the end of every evolution that this Earth allows. I finally believe that we should strive to be the sort of souls that Deity decided at our first formation, and that we should seek for this whichever way that we are shown until we at last attain the supreme spiritual state of PERFECT PEACE PROFOUND, Amen."

However useful formulations of any kind may be

as accessories or props for a faltering faith, they can never be adequate substitutes for a conviction based on actual experience. Someone known to the present author always said when approached by religious people advancing their views: "I don't want any scriptural quotes or to hear about what you think Jesus or anybody else might have said or thought on any occasion. All I want to hear about are your own beliefs based on your own practical experience of life as it happened to you. Those I'll listen to, but anybody else's I won't." In other words, a direct appeal was made for personal experience in preference to unsubstantiated opinions, no matter how highly regarded a source they might come from. It is a good example of the old adage that an ounce of personal experience is worth several tons of untested theory.

Factually the attentive presence of MEMAME is invoked not so much by formal prayers and solemn surroundings as by sincere and meaningful interactions with her influence. Put very simply, she would much rather someone did a small kindly action for another human who needed that attention, or exercised a timely control over their own tempers, than recited a thousand mindless prayers in a room as empty as their emotionless hearts. With MEMAME, feeling for fellow humans means infinitely more than millions of words uttered or mentally mouthed without a trace of inward intentions. She naturally appreciates a thought sent in her direction as much as any woman would, but if it came to choosing between showing the slightest sympathy for another human being in difficulties and listening to the longest paean of praise in her honor from the highest-paid choir in the world, there need be no doubt concerning which would get her wholehearted attention. She is the kind of Woman who would far rather have a ragged bunch of wildflowers given with real love by a little girl than the most magnificent corsage of orchids presented as a social compliment by a multimillionaire. At the same time she might feel insulted as a woman if the millionaire offered her the wilting wildflowers. That would be understandable.

What really matters most to MEMAME is genuine depth of love and feeling in the truest sense of those words. It is a permanent pity that in the English language, which is so incredibly rich in words of multimeaning from almost every other vocabulary, we have so sadly few to describe our most valuable emotion. When it comes to verbally expressing our feelings, we have so few options. We can be fond of something or someone, like them, admire or love them, and few people bother very much to make clear distinctions between the terms. For instance, we say "making love" when we actually mean having sex relations with anyone. If only there were some accepted means of qualifying degrees of love, as there is with, say, wind, which can be measured on a scale from one to ten. Everyone knows that a wind force of one or two would only be a gentle breeze compared with force ten, which is a very severe gale. Could we not adopt a similar scheme, with a scale commencing with a fond attraction and ending with the ultimate: "Greater love hath no man than this, that he will lay down his life for his friend." Such would indeed be the extremity of love for any human alive. It would then be a matter of estimation to say, "I love you strength four or five," depending on the standards decided upon by the majority of humankind to determine the actual degree. Possibly the divisions of such a scale might be decided by the type of sacrifice humans would be willing to make for the sake of attaining a particular degree of love. That, however, might be suspect on the grounds that it would seem too much like purchasing love for fixed prices, which could never be admissible. Nevertheless, there must be some acceptable means of standardizing degrees of love once we know the distinction between minimum and maximum.

Can we genuinely love an ideal? It was once said, "Love the Lord thy God with thine whole heart and thine whole soul and with all thy mind. Then thou shalt love thy neighbor as thyself." That seems to cover the question completely. In fact it should be easier to love an ideal than to love an ordinary human, since we are all well aware of the faults in our own kind, while our ideals should be without these so far as we know to the contrary. So of course it is possible to experience love in connection with an ideal, but to what degree is always questionable. Many mortals have indeed given their lives for their beliefs, preferring to die, often in horrible ways, rather than to renounce their faith, which obviously meant much more to them than living in this world did. Therefore, if beliefs can mean more to some humans than life itself, they are far past being merely valuable, and must plainly be utterly priceless.

That was why early Christians and followers of

most other religions set such a high value on martyrs, believing that martyrdom would immediately cancel out all previous sins and elevate a soul to Heaven instantly, where they would be forthwith crowned with golden glory evermore. It is a matter of historical record that Christians would accost armed soldiers in public places and plead to be killed on the spot because of their faith, even offering considerable sums of cash for the service. If the startled soldier inquired the reason for this extraordinary request, the Christian might reply something like, "You're a Pagan, so you'll go to hell anyway, but I'm a Christian sinner with a lot on my conscience, and if you kill me for my faith I'll go straight to Heaven with all my sins forgiven and have a wonderful time plus a special crown as well. So go ahead and kill me for Christ. You get the money and I get all the glory forever and forevermore, amen." To modern ears this may sound absolutely insane, but there can be no doubt whatever that we have political activists in our times who are perfectly willing to die for what they believe in, which is not even a God or an afterlife of any description. They will not even offer their lives for large sums of money, but purely for political ideas that might well be worthless. Would-be martyrs are always the most dangerous of all fanatics, not only because of what they mean to do, but mostly because of influence their examples have on other humans. It is well said that the blood of martyrs made the firmest foundation for the Church of Christ. In fact, without his own example of martyrdom it is doubtful if the Church would ever have gotten started in the first place.

Nothing strengthens a religious or idealistic faith so much as martyred blood being shed on its behalf, and nothing weakens it more than indifference or ridicule. That is a well-known fact, and it is the main reason why most governments are anxious not to make evident martyrs out of their opponents. Once people can be convinced that some cause is really worth dying for, it will always find faithful adherents, especially amongst young men and women of idealistic inclinations. This is a genetic relic of our Sacred King days long ago, and it is mostly found with those peoples longest accustomed to the practice in Pagan times.

Although our concept of MEMAME may not inspire anyone to an ultimate degree of martyrdom, she should certainly move many to degrees of love beyond tepid ideas of femininity, especially if she can be seen and recognized in other human beings. Yet to what degrees of love are we ever in love with other humans themselves or with our own ideas about them? Who dares decide this definitely? How many humans ever mate with each other because they seem to personify previously held ideas of suitable partners? What man has not imagined his ideal woman and probably masturbated with that idea in his mind? What woman has not formed some ideal image of the man she would like to mate with and possibly done so in her dreams? Some may just imagine in general terms, but others in carefully worked out concepts related with sensual patterns, such as, "My ideal mate would look like so and so, feel like this or that, smell in this particular way, and sound like such and such." Some might even imagine the taste of a kiss to complete the sense picture.

Yet that would only be the commencement of an entire image. More importantly, characteristics must be attributed to this ideal being created in the consciousness. Most of these would naturally be shared by millions with similar needs, such as kindness, sympathy, generosity, honesty, intelligence, and many other similar qualities we normally consider worthwhile and beneficial to humans in general. There also are special skills and abilities appealing to those who especially appreciate them, such as artistic talents, musical or literary qualifications, medical knowledge, or particular talents of any kind. All such would be welcomed with an ideal Being, because those are the factors that make life worth living, and without them what would it be like at all?

Try and imagine if possible a life without ideas whatsoever, or consciousness without the slightest creative ability. It is extremely difficult to begin conceiving of such a state, short of death itself, and there is no certainty about that. Perhaps dreamless sleep might come close to the ideal of idealessness, if there were such a state. Maybe we should satisfy ourselves by imagining a condition of minimum consciousness—simple awareness of only existing, and no more than that. What would that existence be worth by itself? Without that ability to think and imagine things, almost nothing at all. Conversely, if the entire capability of creative consciousness were restored to the full, but without means of expressing it, such a condition would be intolerable for the average human. We must have outlets for our formative faculties, whatever those might be. For the simplest forms of life, movement and nutrition plus reproduction of species should suffice, while the most sophisticated organisms we know of (ourselves) need to express their ideas by every artifice available in order to find self-fulfillment, which is the major goal of every living being from the least to the greatest in the scale of Existence itself. We are all equal in that respect at any rate, for it is the same for a mouse or a man, and is the Holy Grail for which we quest in common.

Relationships with the MEMAME-ideal can differ in one way, depending on whether males or females are making them. In the case of a female, she can be sister, daughter, or friend, but can only be considered as a mate in respect to the male quotient of the female human in question. With males, however, she may be all the relations combined, or separately as seen from either polarity of being. That is to say, a male could see himself only as a mate from the viewpoint of his masculinity quotient, whereas a female human would have to approach a masculine ideal Concept to obtain a similar sexual balance. As humans we may have bisexual natures by many standards, but the purely spiritual concepts of masculine or feminine principles should be seen as representative of their nominal polarities when considered separately. When combined, of course, they become an equalized Energy.

So if fecundity is to occur between humans and Deities on the ideal plane of existence, male humans can inseminate feminine concepts with originative intentions emitted from their masculine polarities, but if they want to conceive ideas on their own accounts, they would have to present the feminine side of themselves toward the masculine concept of Deity for insemination from that spiritual source. It all depends on the purpose for which Deity was being approached in the first place. If only normal and friendly or family contact was desired, either aspect would serve, although distinct needs are associated with either. There are things at which a Mother is best, and other things more appropriate for a Father, and of course sometimes both together can do the most good. This makes the most sensible light in which to approach the Powers whereby we honor our Primal Parents.

If an esoteric exercise is needed to establish a balanced relationship between our idealized Bloodbeings made manifest through ourselves as living beings of either gender, the following format could be very useful. Only the normal requirements of a quiet room and a suitable opportunity is absolutely needed, and all else such as music, incense, lighting, costume, is entirely optional. Attitude of mind and soul is the most important adjunct to obtain, and this exercise should never be done unless the operator is in exactly the right mood to begin with. A few moments of quiet contemplation would be good to start the proceedings with. After that, the verbal and mimetic components can commence while standing before one's chair. Begin by making the Cosmic Cross with the following phrases and actions.

In the name of the Father	Right hand to forehead.
And of the Mother	Left hand to stomach.
And of the Son	Left hand to right shoulder.
And of the Daughter	Right hand to left shoulder.
Amen.	Both hands palms together before breast.
Blessed be the Male	Right hand extended to right. Think male.
And the Female	Left hand extended to left. Think female.
That together	Both hands together center front. Think both.
Make me true.	Hands to sides, slight bow from waist.
He and She am I as We And both of us am I as Me.	Look right left and center with each line.
Come He of Me And be My guiding rod To God.	Sit comfortably, right hand on right knee, and think of male side of self made manifest.
Come She of Me And be My loving Cup To sup.	Left hand on left knee. Think of female side of oneself as Cup of Life to sustain and be filled with experience.

By our blood mating
Together relating
As only love can
Unite woman with man.

Advance hands towards each other while meditating the meaning of meeting. Touch fingertips exploringly and rotate them lightly for a while.

Unite and plight
The troth of both
With heart and soul
Entirely whole.

Push hands together carefully and deliberately, interlocking fingers and thumbs over abdomen.

He
She
Be
Me

Squeeze hands together tightly with each word, relaxing somewhat between pauses. This may be repeated as required with rhythmic motion or as seems suitable until satisfied with self-state.

O Power in me outpour
Make me become much
*   more.*
May all I am increase
Until I meet with peace.

With a final squeeze of hands as tightly as possible, separate them back to each knee with palms down and then relax completely.

So may it always be
With energies in me
To meet and mate
Into a state
Of perfect harmony.

Think over all the previous action and then say this section slowly and with complete sincerity, remembering that it is a prayer.

In the name of the Father
And of the Mother
And of the Son
And of the Daughter
Amen.

Repeat initial procedure.

This is about the briefest and most concise formulary that is capable of conjoining the two polarities of oneself into a single spiritual Concept of practical power. It might always be made more elaborate if really required, but it could scarcely be shortened, since it is already "cut to the bone" so far as essentials are concerned. Modern Western magical methodologies vary considerably from their medieval forerunners, being a great deal more concise and to the immediate point. Moreover, we would not expect invisible energies to become phantoms or objectionable phenomena of any sort, but to work naturally through human or convenient agencies. We have become so accustomed to imperceptible electronic forces acting all around ourselves, which have resulted from our own ideas and thoughts, that magic seems to be only a different and welcome way of working with our consciousness in maybe an unusual manner, but at the same time with every hope of success in the long run, even if much repetition should prove necessary.

There is one important point to bear in mind while we are creating our Mother concept: the percentage of masculinity in it. In theory there should be a quotient of maleness in every female and vice versa, so as to make up a perfect 100 percent Power. So we should not make our ideal Mother *too* feminine, or she will not be anywhere near the perfection point we ought to be aiming at. We have to remember this principle in connection with our Father ideal too, and be careful to include the touch of femininity in his makeup, again being careful not to overdo it, or we shall conclude with infertile homosexual God images. It could be, of course, that our ultimate evolution may turn out to be that of a self-fertilizing species, or auto-reproductive beings like some very humble worms that are male at one end and female at the other. It is possible that we are developing in that direction at present, and in another million years or so the result will be the first types of men-women capable of repeating themselves at need. Such a strange situation may have been what the Sikh dream of a masculine-born Messiah was foreshadowing, and it could have something to do with the unusual increase of homosexuality among males of the present Western world. Many primitive societies, however, were not unduly worried by a minor percentage of feminine male members so long as there were not enough of them to endanger tribal existence. They were simply regarded as infertile females and were treated accordingly. Some of them even gashed themselves on the buttocks every month in order to simulate female menstruation.

It was this monthly loss of blood that was thought to be especially unlucky in ancient times, because it was evidence of female non-pregnancy. Practically all forms of social life in those days revolved around the factors of fecundity for the simple reason that without them humans would be doomed to decay and eventual extinction. That much was obvious to even the meanest intelligence. So everything connected with the factor of fertility was worshipped with honor, and all signs of sterility treated with fear, contempt, and dislike of every kind. Loss of blood from a female body was one of the worst omens possible. Some societies went to the length of supposing that even the shadow of a menstruating woman would bring misfortune to anyone it fell on, and where a plurality of wives was a normal custom, those with the dreaded flow would be banned from approaching their husbands for several days after the event had ceased. It was the loss of blood during childbirth that necessitated a ritual purification some days later, even though it would be regarded as a sign of success and a cause for celebration.

Loss of blood from a man, however, was always seen as something noble if shed in battle, since it was evidence that he had died fighting for something he believed in. Blood has always been a sacred and revered sign amongst humanity, and we shall not breed many millennia of instinctive feelings out of our systems in just a few generations. Therefore we might as well continue to regard blood as something particularly precious amongst humans who are still hoping for an eventual "Salvation," whatever that might amount to on this Earth. It could be the perpetuation of our race on another planet unlucky enough to be a suitable breeding ground for our species, in which case it is to be hoped that only the best possible selection of human bloodstock will be exported from Earth so that the Quest of the Holy Grail can be continued throughout Cosmos with some assurance of ultimate success.

What sort of a success we humans may have made of our Quest during the millennia we have been exhausting the resources of Earth is anyone's guess or opinion. Some might say we have done as well as we could, while others would disagree and point to our obvious and disastrous failures. The truth lies plainly somewhere in between those extremities, and depends entirely upon what standards have been set up to judge by. So far as humanity is concerned, we can only be judged as the sort of souls we have become as men and women, and that again depends on what we have done with ourselves because of the ideals we have adopted and attempted to realize amongst us. Without ideals we could not have reached our current condition of civilization, however unsatisfactory this may seem to critics of general human conduct. On the other hand, if ideals have led us into our present position, can they not continue leading us out of it into some far better state of being beyond the boundaries of this world entirely? That indeed is the only hope we have to hang on to with all our might.

In extremely primitive times our only chance of survival lay in hanging on to our mother's hair as close to her breast as possible. Thus we had some assurance of food, shelter, and protection. If we lost our grip and our mothers could not pick us up and re-apply us, we were finished. What was once true as a physical fact is now true as a psychological one, and as a principle we cannot ignore with impunity. If we lost our grip on our Mother ideal, we shall perish for the want of those mental and spiritual equivalents of milk with which she alone can nourish us. Our Father ideal may supply the seed that commences a Concept within our feminine psyches, but once we have brought it to birth as an actuality amongst us, it will depend on how well it can be applied to the breast of our Mother ideals for food, enabling it to mature and grow into substantial significance according to our standards of appreciation.

Therefore we need to think of our idealized

Bloodbeing not only as Someone with the power of conceiving and bringing our ideas to birth, but Someone who is also capable of caring for them until they will be able to look after themselves. While the masculine quotient in ourselves may germinate any concepts we might produce in this life, it will always be the feminine constituent of human nature that will have to not only gestate them but also feed and assist their future growth and development once they have appeared as a viable creature of consciousness. It was once told of Michael Faraday, inventor of the dynamo, that after he had given a lecture-demonstration of it, a lady in the audience asked politely, "Can the professor please tell us the use of his pretty little toy?" Whereupon Faraday replied with equal courtesy, "Certainly madam, if you will be good enough to tell us the use of a new-born baby." That was the perfect answer then and now.

No one can possibly tell what use any of us are until maybe the end of our lives, and probably not even then, since something we have said or done during those lives may have influenced another person to do something dramatic or significant in the course of their incarnations. We are still being influenced by people who died physically some several thousand years ago, since their recorded thoughts are yet current amongst us and we have altered ourselves however minutely in consequence. Who will ever know the bloodlines that connect us all through one field of consciousness after another, reaching right back into the womb of Time itself? If we like to think of it as serialized sex through the centuries, there is no reason why we shouldn't.

Probably few modern people would doubt that our present period belongs more to women than to men. In former times fair ladies were asking their noble knights to draw their swords and kill each other in the cause of whatever they believed was best. Now that those swords have become nuclear ones, we need the descendants of those bloodthirsty ladies to demand all weapons be safely sheathed on pain of the worst punishments they can think of. If only our politicians were still small children, their mothers might control such diabolical inclinations with a slipper or the palm of a hand applied smartly to bared buttocks. What a pity it is that the womenfolk of perverse politicians and other organizers of warfare do not threaten the same procedures today, preferably with worldwide TV coverage. The mere possibility of such a shame-making show becoming public property forever should deter the biggest of the bomb-happy brigade from pressing the blast-button. The vital question here is whether the concerted will of all the worthwhile women in this world can be strong enough to prevent their menfolk from destroying themselves and their children beyond any hope of reconstitution.

There was once a small African tribe that became taken into total captivity by a larger and much more powerful one. Realizing their complete helplessness in the clutch of their captors, and feeling the loss of their freedom as keenly as they did, those unwilling slaves decided amongst themselves to take the only possible course of action they could. They refused to breed and thus provide their hated conquerors with ready-made second generation servitors. Any children accidentally born were smothered at birth, though normally the women simply refused to let their men have fertile intercourse with them. They valued their independence so highly that they preferred perishing as a people rather than remaining on Earth as captive chattels of oppressive owners. Since it was a very small tribe of only a few families to start with, the entire lot of them were extinct in due course. What an example of emancipation at the cost of posterity! It is assumed that their existing children at the time of their initial capture were either forcibly sterilized by their parents or persuaded against propagating themselves by some powerful prohibition. Following the last two World Wars, how many humans refused to have families who might be slaughtered in future ones? What genetic genius and amazing inventiveness have been lost on that account? No one will ever know.

At a news conference after the last World War, some journalist asked an American general how he thought the next one would be fought. The general replied, "I can't answer that question, but I can tell you for a certainty about the weaponry of the war after that one." The writer fell for this and inquired what those weapons might consist of in the general's opinion. That officer replied promptly and grimly, "It'll be fought with bows and arrows. Maybe some of the soldiers will have spears as well!" How horribly true that telling remark might become may we never discover for a certainty. Nevertheless, could it come equally true that our future fate will lie more in the hands of our women than our menfolk? Let us hope for the sake of our humanity that this might indeed be so.

However, there must always be one proviso with such a sincere wish. That is, may only the best and most motherly side of female nature be considered as a model for basing our idealistic beliefs upon. The worst side of womanhood, as depicted by oldtime demons like Lilith or Nehamah and our modern female terrorists, should be excluded from our conscious calculations by every possible exorcism we can think of. Lilith was the fabled first, or "pre-Eve," wife of Adam who bore him nothing but demons, since she mated with the worst side of his nature and so represented bad blood and poor genetics. Legend says that God removed her when he saw the results of such mismating and substituted Eve, who bore him ordinary human children instead, thus affording some hopes for their future development. Nehamah was a demon who delighted in the deaths of the newly born, which she was said to devour with relish. Today we call her the infant mortality rate, and yet strictly speaking it is better that she should claim the children of Lilith rather than that they should grow up and become fully fledged fiends having horrible effects all around them. This world would be an improved place without them.

We would dearly like to believe that this could indeed be possible in time—if we have enough of it left—and that old War Goddesses like Bellona, the sister-wife of Mars with her wild and horrible appearance, might be transmuted by the wills of well-intentioned women into our benign and blessed Bloodmother known under so many other names and descriptions. However we call her, she would never want her children to destroy themselves for such stupid and sometimes ridiculous reasons. She would much rather sacrifice them with her own hands, and maybe she will be forced to do so yet if we refuse to learn our lessons any other way. Far better that we should perish from plagues and natural diseases than murder our fellow mortals for the sake of proving how powerful any pathetic survivors might be.

We are certainly facing a fatal age. Another millennium of the Christian calendar, and the last one brought the bloody battles of religious intolerance and opportunism. Again let us hope those horrors will not be repeated on social or political levels in our era. Last time, Western womenfolk were urging their men to go out and kill everyone else who did not agree with their religious opinions. This time let us pray that all our women will forbid fighting of any description in the name of the Goddess they once stood for and should represent today more strongly than ever. If they all spoke clearly and loudly enough with Her voice, who knows, men might *have* to listen and even obey because they would realize their Mother was commanding them. If only we could survive the next century in comparative peace, we might, just *might* stand a reasonable chance of social and spiritual safety. Which again could provide our highest and perhaps our only hope of finally fulfilling our Divine destiny in

PERFECT PEACE PROFOUND.

BETWEEN GOOD AND EVIL
by William G. Gray
If you are seeking Inner Light, read this important new book. *Between Good and Evil* provides new insight that can help you take the forces of Darkness that naturally exist within us and transform them into spirtual light. This book will help you discover how you can deal constructively, rather than destructively, with the unavoidable problem of Evil. Our lives depend on which way we direct our energy—whether we make the Devil in ourselves serve the God, or the other way around. We must use our Good intentions to understand and exploit the Evil energies that would otherwise prove fatal to us.

In order to confront and control our "demons," Gray has revived a centuries-old magical ritual technique called the *Abramelin Experience:* a practical, step-by-step process in which you call upon your Holy Guardian Angel to assist in converting Evil into Good. By following the richly detailed explanation of this "spiritual alchemy," you will learn how to positively channel your negative energies into a path leading directly to a re-union with Divinity.

The power of altering your future lies in your own hands, and within this unique book you will discover the means to move forward in your spiritual evolution. You will find the principles discussed in this multi-faceted book valuable and insightful.
0-87542-273-X, 304 pgs., 5¼ × 8, softcover   **$9.95**

TEMPLE MAGIC
William Gray
This important book on occultism deals specifically with problems and details you are likely to encounter in temple practice. Learn how a temple should look, how a temple should function, what a ceremonialist should wear, what physical postures best promote the ideal spiritual-mental attitude, and how magic is worked in a temple.

Temple Magic has been written specifically for the instruction and guidance of esoteric ceremonialists by someone who has spent a lifetime in spiritual service to his natural Inner Way. There are few comparable works in existence, and this book in particular deals with up-to-date techniques of constructing and using a workable temple dedicated to the furtherance of the Western Inner Tradition. In simple yet adequate language, it helps any individual understand and promote the spiritual structure of our esoteric inheritance. It is a book by a specialist for those who are intending to be specialists.
0-87542-274-8, 240 pages, 5¼ x 8, illus., softcover   **$7.95**

THE NEW MAGUS
by Donald Tyson

The New Magus is a practical framework on which a student can base his or her personal system of magic.

This book is filled with practical, usable magical techniques and rituals which anyone from any magical tradition can use. It includes instructions on how to design and perform rituals, create and use sigils, do invocations and evocations, do spiritual healings, learn rune magic, use god-forms, create telesmatic images, discover your personal guardian, create and use magical tools and much more. You will learn how *YOU* can be a *New Magus!*

The New Age is based on ancient concepts that have been put into terms, or *metaphors*, that are appropriate to life in our world today. That makes *The New Magus* the book on magic for today.

If you have found that magic seems illogical, overcomplicated and not appropriate to your lifestyle, *The New Magus* is the book for you. It will change your ideas of magic forever!

0-87542-825-8, 6 x 9, illus., softcover.   **$12.95**

THE GOLDEN DAWN
by Israel Regardie

The Original Account of the Teachings, Rites and Ceremonies of the Hermetic Order of the Golden Dawn as revealed by Israel Regardie, with further revision, expansion, and additional notes by Israel Regardie, Cris Monnastre, and others.

Originally published in four bulky volumes of some 1200 pages, this 5th Revised and Enlarged Edition has been entirely reset in modern, less space-consuming type, in half the pages (while retaining the original pagination in marginal notation for reference) for easier use.

Corrections of typographical errors perpetuated in the original and subsequent editions have been made, with further revision and additional text and notes by actual practitioners of the Golden Dawn system of Magick, with an Introduction by the only student ever accepted for personal training by Regardie.

Also included are Initiation Ceremonies, important rituals for consecration and invocation, methods of meditation and magical working based on the Enochian Tablets, studies in the Tarot, and the system of Qabalistic Correspondences that unite the World's religions and magical traditions into a comprehensive and practical whole.

This volume is designed as a study and practice curriculum suited to both group and private practice. Meditation upon, and following with the Active Imagination, the Initiation Ceremonies is fully experiential without need of participation in group or lodge.

0-87542-663-8, 744 pages, 6 x 9, illus.   **$19.95**

MYSTERIA MAGICA
by Denning and Phillips

For years, Denning and Phillips headed the international occult Order Aurum Solis. In this book they present the magickal system of the order so that you can use it. Here you will find rituals for banishing and invoking plus instructions for proper posture and breathing. You will learn astral projection, rising on the planes, and the magickal works that should be undertaken through astral projection. You will learn the basic principle of ceremonies and how to make sigils and talismans. You will learn practical Enochian magick plus how to create, consecrate and use your magickal tools such as the magickal sword, wand and cup. You will also learn the advanced arts of sphere-working and evocation to visible appearance.

Filled with illustrations, this book is an expanded version of the previous edition. It is now complete in itself and can be the basis of an entire magickal system. You can use the information alone or as the sourcebook for a group. It is volume 3 of **The Magical Philosophy**, the other two books being *The Sword and The Serpent* and *The Foundations of High Magick*. If you want to learn how to do real magick, this is the place you should start.

0-87542-196-2, 480 pgs., 6 x 9, illus., softcover $15.00

THE SWORD AND THE SERPENT: The Magical Structure
of Cosmos and Psyche
Being a revision and expansion of Books III and IV of the first edition.
by Denning and Phillips

This is the comprehensive guide to the Magical Qabalah with extensive correspondences as well as the techniques for activating the centers, use of images and the psychology of attainment.

In this volume, histories from contemporary life together with references to the works of mystics, poets, artists, philosophers and authorities in psychology are cited to illustrate point by point the action and interaction of the functions of the psyche as identified in Qabalistic teaching.

In this book is set forth clearly the real meaning of adepthood: in relation to this, frequent enigmas of occult literature such as the Abyss, the Knowledge and Conversation of the Holy Guardian Angel, and the supernal attainments, are presented in their true meaning and significance. The natural dignity and potential of life in this world is your birthright. In this volume, its splendor and power are made unmistakably manifest.

0-87542-197-0, 512 pgs., 6 x 9, illus., softcover $15.00

THE NATURE AND USE OF RITUAL
by Dr. Peter Roche de Coppens

The New Age is not a time or place, but a *new state of consciousness*. To bring about this new consciousness, we need a viable source of revelation and teaching that gets to the heart of our Being and Reality: a way of living and seeing that leads to a gradual, organic and holistic (or 'holy') transformation of the present consciousness and being.

The basic aim of this book is to render explicit the essence of this process of *bio-psycho-spiritual* transformation in terms of our own indigenous Spiritual Tradition, which we can find in the very basic Christian Prayers and Documents.

Perhaps at no time in history has the need for new consciousness been greater — if indeed we are to survive and fulfill our destiny and the Divine potential that is seeded within each person.

At no time has the opportunity been greater, for access to the highest esoteric knowledge, the most refined spiritual technology, is now available to bring about the transformation of consciousness on a massive scale—only if each of us accepts this goal as our personal responsibility.
0-87542-675-1, 229 pages, softcover, illus.   **$9.95**

THE INVISIBLE TEMPLE
By Peter Roche de Coppens

The Invisible Temple is not a building or location. It is not a particular congregation of people. It *is* wherever there is a focal point for spiritual energy. It is located where that energy is generated, amplified and transformed for whatever purpose is needed. In other words, The Invisible Temple exists for us when we become a spiritual light generator.

In the tradition of Regardie's *The Middle Pillar,* this book shows how you can generate, transform and amplify spiritual energy. But it goes further by showing how this can be done with a group of people, making a spiritual light generator that is almost beyond comprehension!

Filled with illustrations and exercises, this book gives occult techniques for spiritual attainment within a largely mystic Christian framework (but with constant reference to other traditions to show the universality of the techniques themselves). It can easily be used by Christians, Jews, Pagans and any others on a spiritual path. The structure of the book is also Qabalistic, and the symbols and rituals were actually drawn from a Qabalistic Tradition. Here is a book that can truly help you to live magically!
0-87542-676-X, 300 pages, illustrated, 5¼" x 8," softcover.   **$9.95**

THE LLEWELLYN PRACTICAL GUIDE TO
THE DEVELOPMENT OF PSYCHIC POWERS
by Denning & Phillips

You may not realize it, but .. you already have the ability to use ESP, Astral Vision and Clairvoyance, Divination, Dowsing, Prophecy, Communication with Spirits, Mental Telepathy, etc. It's simply a matter of knowing what to do, and then to exercise (as with any talent) and develop them. Written by two of the most knowledgeable experts in the world of Magick today, this book is a complete course—teaching you, step-by-step, how to develop these powers that actually have been yours since birth. Using the techniques they teach, you will soon be able to move objects at a distance, see into the future, know the thoughts and feelings of another person, find lost objects, locate water and even people using your own no-longer-latent talents.

Psychic powers are as much a natural ability as any other talent. You'll learn to play with these new skills, work with groups of friends to accomplish things you never would have believed possible before reading this book. The text shows you how to make the equipment you can use, the exercises you can do, and how to use your abilities to change your life and the lives of those close to you. Many of the exercises can be adapted as games for pleasure and fun, as well as development.

0-87542-191-1, 256 pgs., 5¼ x 8, illus., softcover $7.95

THE LLEWELLYN PRACTICAL GUIDE TO ASTRAL PROJECTION
by Denning & Phillips

Yes, your consciousness can be sent forth, out-of-the-body, with full awareness and return with full memory. You can travel through time and space, converse with non-physical entities, obtain knowledge by non-material means, and experience higher dimensions.

Is there life-after-death? Are we forever shackled by time & space? The ability to go forth by means of the Astral Body, or Body of Light, gives the personal assurance of consciousness (and life) beyond the limitations of the physical body. The requisite practices are set forth in step-by-step procedures, augmented with photographs and put-you-in-the-picture visualization aids. Great benefits from the various practices themselves are demonstrated in renewed physical and emotional health, mental discipline, spiritual attainment, and the development of extra faculties.

Guidance is also given to the Astral World itself: what to expect, what can be done—including the ecstatic experience of Astral Sex between two people who project together into this higher world where true union is consummated free of the barriers of physical bodies.

0-87542-181-4, 272 pgs., 5¼ x 8, illus., softcover $7.95